STILL FIGURING IT OUT

Lea Gorf

STILL FIGURING IT OUT

What it really means to
be twenty-something

Not a self-help book, a self-discovery book
for the ones still figuring it out

Lea Gorf

STILL FIGURING IT OUT

This book is a work of creative nonfiction. Some names and identifying details have been changed to protect privacy. The views and reflections expressed are based on personal experience and observation.

First Edition, Janurary 2026
10 9 8 7 6 5 4 3 2 1
ISBN (Print): 978-0-646-73344-9
ISBN (eBook): 978-0-646-73184-1

Front cover design by Lea Gorf
Back cover design by B.G.Design
Typesetting by B.G.Design
Edited by: Tayler Hill
Printed in Australia by Ingram Spark

Published in Australia by Lea Gorf Publishing
All enquiries: lea@leagorf.com

LEA'S DISCLAIMER

This book serves educational and reflective purposes. The author presents personal perspectives, experiences, and interpretations. The content does not provide psychological, medical, or professional advice and does not substitute qualified professional support. Readers should seek independent professional guidance where appropriate. Any resemblance to actual persons, living or deceased, remains coincidental unless explicitly stated. The author and publisher disclaim all responsibility for any loss, risk, or liability, personal or otherwise, incurred directly or indirectly because of the use or interpretation of the content of this book.

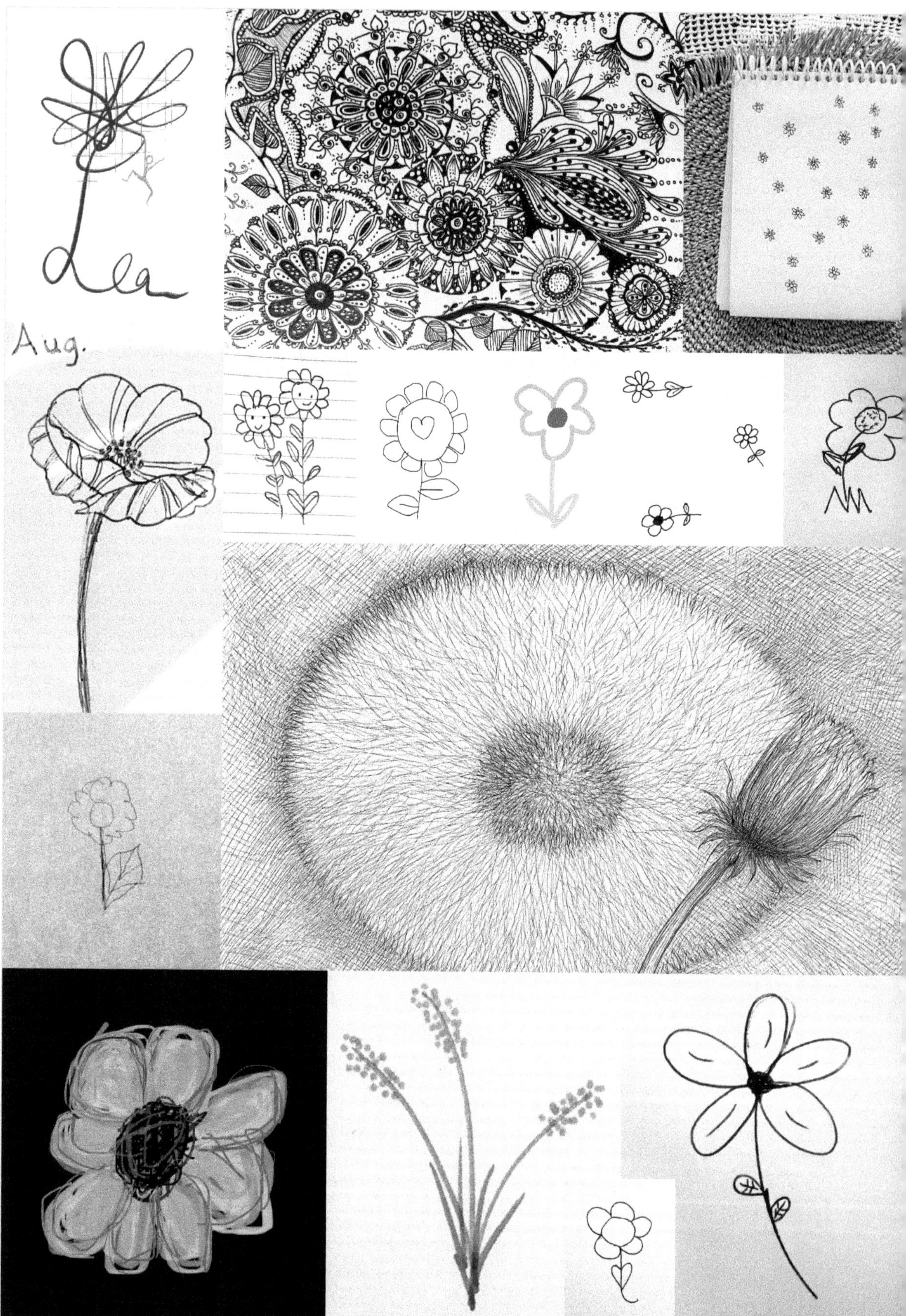
Lea
Aug.

“

If you do not ask,
or talk to your community,
you will not build one.

”

Lea Gorf

CONTENTS

VI *SHIFTS AND SHADOWS*

VII *THE REAL WORLD*

VIII *LESSONS AND LAUGHS*

IX *THE TURNING POINT*

X *NOTES TO SELF*

ABSTRACT

BEING TWENTY-SOMETHING IS NOT A FIXED DECADE. It is the messy, beautiful middle of becoming. It feels like standing in the middle of a crowded intersection where every direction seems possible, yet none come with clear instructions. Social media screams for attention, milestones seem to arrive either too late or too soon, and conversations often dissolve into distractions. The pandemic bent time, travel accelerated growth, and body image became an ongoing negotiation between self-perception and outside judgment.

This book began on an ordinary night, a balcony conversation that stretched until sunrise. No one had it all together. One was job-hunting, another recovering from heartbreak, another planning to leave the country. Between laughter and tears, someone said, "*I thought by now I'd have it figured out.*"

The silence that followed, turned into laughter because it was true for everyone there. Still Figuring It Out was born from that moment of shared honesty. It is not a manual with clear steps, but a mirror reflecting the confusion, humour, and quiet courage of being in your twenties. It does not hand out perfect answers. Instead, it captures the in-between: not yet settled, not completely lost either.

Through stories, reflections, and Pause & Think moments, my book explores what it means to live, question, and stumble through early adulthood from doom scrolling and communication breakdowns to gender dynamics, body image, and the strange relativity of age. Each chapter blends my personal reflection with interactive exercises, inviting pause, laughter, and recognition.

The goal is not to fix life, it's to see it closely, curiously, and with a sense of humour about being human. Ultimately, *Still Figuring It Ou*t is a companion for anyone juggling the chaos and beauty of growing up. It offers resonance instead of resolution, relief instead of rules, and the gentle reminder that uncertainty does not mean failure, it means you are alive, learning, and exactly where you need to be.

"Maybe age is just something we feel."

PROLOGUE

IT IS 01:04 A.M. IN AUSTRALIA, AND THE SILENCE outside feels heavier than the thoughts running through my mind. Hyper-focus has a way of sneaking in during these hours, making space for questions that refuse to stay quiet: *Why am I here? What do I want? How did life become so beautifully messy and confusing at the same time?*

My brother at home has just become a father with a woman who embodies chaos, and as a result, his son has become a miracle. Friends are spread across countries and time zones, their voices reaching me through calls that never align perfectly but always remind me of belonging. Relationships stretch across distance and years, testing patience and loyalty while redefining what it means to commit.

And in the middle of it all, there is me. Awake at a time when the world expects sleep, wondering if this restless energy might hold a purpose. That is when the fragments of this book began to take shape, half-thoughts, half-questions, all circling what it means to be twenty-something. This may be the moment to start piecing together the fragments: the fears, the lessons, the raw honesty of being twenty-something - a decade defined, less by answers and more by the courage to ask.

I came to the realisation that we are just humans, especially in our twenties. COVID-19 shifted so much in how we interact, how we connect, and how we measure time. It left me wondering: *Is there even such a thing as age? Some say I look twenty-one, others call me old because I am 27 years old, but isn't age simply how we feel in a given moment?*

Travel has deepened that thought. Moving through countries matures more than it ages, not in appearance but in resilience. There are moments when it feels overwhelming, when mistakes and setbacks weigh heavily. Yet at other times, gratitude surfaces for the lessons learned, for the growth that only difficult experiences create. Each of these interaction shapes not only perspective but also the sense of time itself.

This is what this book is about: the search for meaning in being twenty-something, maybe even thirty, forty, or beyond. It's about the strange mix of chaos and clarity, of fear and growth, which defines these years. It's an invitation to explore what it really means to be in the middle of becoming. I do not have all the answers, but I hope you will enjoy reading this book as much as I enjoyed writing it.

> I CRIED, WISHING I WAS OLDER. NOW I WISH I COULD BE A KID AGAIN. MAYBE GROWING UP IS JUST MISSING THE OTHER SIDE.

HOW TO READ THIS BOOK

THIS BOOK DOES NOT FOLLOW A SINGLE CORRECT reading path. The chapters reflect overlapping experiences rather than linear phases. Some sections may seem immediately relevant, while others may resonate later. Reading in the order provided offers a narrative arc from noise and confusion to clarity and self-confidence. Selective reading allows you to return to topics as your life changes.

The "Pause & Think" moments, reflection exercises, and quiz questions serve as interruptions rather than tasks. Reflection can take the form of writing, silent contemplation or recognition. Repetition is intentional. Revisiting the same questions at different times makes changes more visible than reaching conclusions. My book serves as a companion rather than a guide. The meaning arise through interaction rather than instruction.

INTRODUCTION

BEING TWENTY-SOMETHING FEELS LIKE STANDING IN the middle of a crowded intersection where every direction seems possible, yet none come with clear instructions. Social media screams for attention, milestones seem to arrive late or too soon, and conversations often dissolve into distractions. The pandemic bent time, travel accelerated growth, and body image remains an ongoing negotiation between self-perception and outside judgment. My book grew out of the noise in my own head. I talk a lot, think a lot, listen a lot. My mind is restless and often overstimulated, yet curious and alive. I have always tried to understand where we stand in life, especially in our twenties. Along the way, I realised that I am not alone in this search. My book explores what it means to live, question, and stumble through the shifting scenery of early adulthood. Each chapter should feel like a friend thinking out loud, yet read like an author who knows exactly what she says. I am writing about doom scrolling, communication breakdowns, gender dynamics, body image, and the strange relativity of age.

Ageing is a funny thing. Some marry at twenty-one or thirty-something, others never at all. Some start families in their twenties, while others do so in their thirties or later. There is no proper timeline, only individual paths that somehow weave into this collective story of becoming. For me, the realisation of growing up came in small, ordinary moments. Suddenly, I liked olives. Dark chocolate tasted better than milk chocolate. Drama lost its charm. Looking at my mom, who is no longer 36 years old. Friends and strangers started calling me old. There are indeed times I feel old, like when nostalgia sneaks up in a song or a film. Then I remember the days I cried on my mother's and father's shoulder, wishing to be older, desperate to understand life, or to wear makeup because being grown-up seemed glamorous. Now, I sometimes wish I could be a child again, if only for the joy of eating whatever I wanted, whenever I wanted.

Also, being born between the '90s and the '00s, is that my generation grew up without technology, yet also in, yet also grew up with an in-between space that makes time feel slippery. Movies I thought came out a few years ago turn out to be fifteen or twenty years old. Horton Hears a Who was released in 2008, and somehow that still feels recent. Whereas Hannah Montana, Zoey 101, and Phineas and Ferb feel like a lifetime ago. Therefore, each chapter blends my stories, insights, and interactive exercises together to invite you too pause, giggle, and give you honest confrontation moments. The goal is not to solve life but to observe it closely and laugh with recognition at being human.

While you read this book, take a moment to breathe in and out, stretch, and check your posture. Read slowly, with curiosity. Let these reflections remind you that you are not behind, not too much, and not alone, you are, like all of us, still figuring it out. Everyone, in their own way, is still figuring it out. That recognition is not heavy or hopeless, it is freeing. It means there is space to laugh, to stumble, and to grow without needing to have all the answers yet.

THINK & PAUSE

How did you know you were growing up or becoming an adult?

Was it in small shifts like food preferences and music, or in bigger moments like moving away, paying bills, or saying goodbye?

MEET TWENTY-SOMETHING

TWENTY-SOMETHING IS NOT A PERSON, NOT REALLY. More like a houseguest who shows up uninvited, drops their backpack on the floor, and makes themselves at home in your life. They talk too loudly sometimes, oversleep or under-sleep other times, keep you up at night wondering, and constantly ask questions you do not know how to answer.

Some days, twenty-something feels like your best friend pushing you to book that flight, say yes to the unknown, laugh too hard, and love too much. Other days, they feel like your worst critic whispering that you are behind, comparing you to everyone else, and reminding you that everyone else has it figured out, except reminding you that no one has it figured out besides you.

The thing about twenty-something is: they do not care about numbers. You might meet them at eighteen, staring at the ceiling in your childhood bedroom as the weight of your future settles on your shoulders. Wondering what comes next, what path you're supposed to commit to for the rest of your life. Or at twenty-nine, sitting in a job interview that makes you wonder if you have been on the wrong path all along. Some even bump into them later, at thirty-five or forty, when life throws a curveball that sends them right back to the same questions:

Who am I? What am I doing? Where do I belong?

Everyone meets twenty-something at some point. The only difference is when.

WHAT DOES BEING TWENTY-SOMETHING MEAN TO YOU?

FOR ME, IT'S THE IN-BETWEEN OF EVERYTHING, THE years that stretch and fold, where certainty feels far away but possibility feels close enough to touch. It's waking up one day and realising you have quietly grown into a version of yourself you did not even notice arriving. It's the small moments of courage between decisions, the laughter that hides confusion, and the quiet realisations that reshape everything. Being twenty-something is not a straight line. It's a collage of lessons and detours, the years where friendships grow, dreams shift, and self-understanding deepens in unexpected ways. It's about unlearning what no longer fits and allowing yourself to rebuild without apology.

Some days, it feels like everything is happening all at once. Other days, nothing moves at all. And maybe that is the point that these years are not meant to be figured out perfectly, but felt deeply. To be twenty-something is to exist between becoming and belonging, between trying to find meaning and learning to create it.

Maybe it isn't about finding all the answers.

Maybe it is about learning to ask better questions.

WHAT KIND OF TWENTY-SOMETHING ARE YOU?

If your twenties were a weather forecast, what would it be:

a) Stormy with sunshine breaks
b) A long, confusing fog
c) A heatwave you did not pack for
d) Four seasons in one day

Which survival kit item fits your twenties best?

a) Noise-cancelling headphones
b) A giant coffee mug
c) A suitcase with broken wheels
d) A journal full of scribbles

Pick your twenties soundtrack:

a) "On Top of the World"
b) "Lost in Translation"
c) "Work in Progress"
d) All of the Above

What is your guiding motto?

a) Fake it till you make it
b) One step at a time
c) Everything happens for a reason
d) Who even knows?

RESULTS

Mostly A's — *Stormy with Sunshine Breaks*

You are an optimist with realism. Life feels unpredictable, but you have learned to dance between chaos and clarity. You do not avoid the storm; you should have just packed better shoes.

> *SURVIVAL ITEM:* **Noise-cancelling headphones** because not every opinion deserves space in your head.

Mostly B's — *A Long, Confusing Fog*

You are in the discovery phase. Not lost, just searching. You move more slowly, think more deeply, and trust that clarity will arrive when it is ready. Your strength is reflection, not rush.

> *SURVIVAL ITEM:* **Giant coffee mug** you run on caffeine and hope, but you still show up.

Mostly C's — *A Heatwave You Did Not Pack For*

You are in an intense growth era. Everything feels too much, but it is shaping you. You are learning not to mistake discomfort for failure.

> *SURVIVAL ITEM:* **Suitcase with broken wheels**, you are still moving, even when things fall apart.

Mostly D's — *Four Seasons in One Day*

You embody the full twenty-something spectrum. Joy and doubt, ambition and rest, chaos, and calm all in rotation.

> NO MATTER YOUR ANSWERS, YOU ARE DOING FINE. THE TWENTIES ARE NOT MEANT TO BE MASTERED; THEY ARE MEANT TO BE LIVED.

I

FIGURING IT OUT

The noise, chaos, questions, and contradictions of being twenty-something.

AM I GOING CRAZY, OR IS THE WORLD GOING CRAZY?

SANITY IS RELATIVE WHEN THE FEED NEVER ENDS. Sometimes it feels like the ground under reality has shifted, just slightly, but enough to make everything feel off. You wake up, scroll on your phone, and before your feet even touch the floor, the world is already loud. Bad news. Opinions. Updates. Someone else's perfect life. Someone else's panic. Someone else's urgency. It never really stops.

There are days when I catch myself wondering how this became normal, walking somewhere without checking a screen, eating without documenting it, and sitting in silence without filling it. Things that once felt natural now feel almost strange, like habits from another lifetime. And that's when the question creeps in quietly: **Am I crazy, or is the world going crazy?**

I don't think humans suddenly changed. I think we adapted too fast. Our brains weren't built for this much information, this many inputs, this constant sense of "stay alert." We're processing headlines, which are meant to shock us, notifications intended to pull us back in, and pressure to always respond, always know, always react. No wonder our thoughts feel jumpy. No wonder focusing feels harder. No wonder rest feels earned instead of allowed.

Sometimes it feels like collective overstimulation. Like we're all running on a slightly fried nervous system and pretending it's fine. The constant scrolling. The half-listening. The need for noise even when we're exhausted. It can feel a bit... unhinged.

And when your own thoughts start racing, it's easy to turn inward and assume something is wrong with you. But here's the thing that grounds me: *it's not just you. It's not just me.* We're all swimming in the same noise. The anxiety you feel isn't always personal, sometimes it's environmental. Sometimes what feels like inner chaos is just your mind reacting to a world that doesn't slow down. Realising that shifts something. It softens the self-blame.

Instead of asking, "*What's wrong with me?*" the question becomes, "*What am I responding to?*"

And often, the answer is simple: **too much. Too fast. Too loud.**

So if your thoughts feel scattered, if your attention slips, if you feel overwhelmed by things you can't quite name, it doesn't mean you're broken. It means you're human, living inside a system that wasn't designed with human limits in mind.

And if you're up for it, let's do a small, gentle check-in. Nothing serious. No diagnosis. Just a moment to notice where you're at in the middle of all this daily madness.

RATE YOUR LEVEL OF DAILY MADNESS

When waking up, the first action is:

(a) Check the phone at once
(b) Breathe, stretch, then check the phone
(c) Leave the phone until later

Scrolling time each day feels like:

(a) A black hole with no escape
(b) A habit, sometimes useful, some times numbing
(c) A tool, used with limits

Conversations with friends often involve:

(a) Talking about social media content
(b) A mix of online references and real-life stories
(c) Barely any mention of feeds or trends

The thought I might be losing it comes:

(a) Daily
(b) Sometimes
(c) Rarely

RESULTS

Mostly A's — *Living in noise*

If your day begins and ends with a screen, it doesn't mean you're failing, it means your mind is overloaded and looking for a way out. I've been there too. There were weeks when I sat in front of a screen for eight hours a day and still told myself I was "too busy" to slow down. I scrolled through other people's lives until I couldn't feel my own anymore. Every quiet moment felt uncomfortable, so I filled it with noise. The truth is, you're not losing your mind, you're overwhelmed, and your phone has become the easiest way to get out of your head.

TRY THIS:

- Delay your first scroll by 5–10 minutes.
- Swap one doom-scroll session for a walk, a stretch, or literally staring out the window.
- Turn off notifications you don't need (i.e. most of them)

Small changes alleviate the chaos, they may not solve all your problems, but they give your mind room to breathe again.

Mostly B's — *Half in Reality, Half in the Feed*

You're aware of the noise, but not entirely out of it. You dip in and out sometimes scrolling with intention, other times out of habit. This was me for years: telling myself social media wasn't that bad, while wondering why my anxiety spiked whenever I put the phone down. I used my phone to distract myself from feelings I didn't want to sit with: boredom, sadness, loneliness, uncertainty. Your mind isn't chaotic, it's overstimulated. You crave peace, but you also crave escape.

TRY THIS:

- Notice what emotion you feel right before you grab your phone.
- Keep your phone in another room for one task (shower, laundry, cooking)
- Schedule one "offline hour" a day, no rules, just presence.

This is the level where awareness becomes change.

Mostly C's — *Both feet firmly on the ground, clear head*

If you hardly think about your smartphone and your world seems bigger than your screen, you are in a healthy rhythm. But staying grounded is still an exercise, because life is loud and the digital world is just waiting to pull you back in.

TRY THIS:

- Protect the routines that keep you calm.
- Don't underestimate how quickly chaos can return when boundaries fade.
- Let yourself be proud, living in the real world is rare these days.

Your peace is intentional, not accidental.

MY STORY

For a long time, I used my mobile phone to escape my own thoughts. Scrolling was easier for me than feeling. Notifications distracted me from the heaviness I didn't want to face, but the more I reached for my phone, the more disconnected I felt, from myself, from other people, from the present moment. My life was wonderful, but I hardly lived it. I didn't stop spending time in front of the screen overnight. I didn't need a digital detox, I just needed gentler habits. One small step at a time:

- I stopped checking my mobile phone as soon as I woke up.
- I left it in another room while I ate.
- I replaced "filling the silence" with "listening to it.

And slowly, the noise grew quieter, my thoughts grew calmer, and reality felt real again. Experiencing the here and now didn't happen suddenly, but in tiny moments, moments when I didn't flee, moments when I chose myself over the screen.

VALIDATION

You are not crazy.
You are not broken.
You are not weak because you feel overwhelmed.

We all live in a world that demands us to be connected, entertained, available, and productive at the same time. If it's noisy in your head, it's because the world is loud. And learning to turn down that volume, even if only slightly, is an act of self-respect.

DOOM SCROLLING

THE BLACK HOLE OF TIME

THERE'S LITERALLY A TERM FOR DOOM-SCROLLING now: brain-rotting. It is both sad and strangely funny that something so numbing has been given its own name. If you pause long enough to notice, it becomes frightening how much time dissolves into screens and how easily we sacrifice even more of it just to feel a little less overwhelmed. Social media rarely feels harmful at the moment, but its effects are profound. Attention spans swindles, motivation fades, and even replying to a message from a loved one can take 1-14 business days, but somehow, we always find time to scroll.

Doom scrolling creeps into the smallest moments, on the bus, between tasks, when trying to rest, replacing silence with stimulation. My kiwi friend Sara once told me that she had closed an app only to reopen it seconds later without realising. This confession stuck with me, perhaps because I have done the same thing hundreds of times. Hours pass unnoticed. The brain loves loops, short-term dopamine, and maybe that's why resting now feels like work.

The real questions are:

Do you pick up your phone to relax, only to lose yourself in endless feeds?

Does a quick glance quietly turn into an hour before you even realise it?

Our phones have become the background noise of our twenties. Always buzzing. Always within reach. Always offering a small escape from everything that feels unsettled. When life feels uncertain, heavy, or undefined, the phone promises relief without commitment. No decisions. No answers. Just something to fill the space.

We reach for it to rest, but somehow, we end up more tired. A glance becomes a spiral. The uncertainty, pressure, loneliness, and constant comparison that shape this decade make the escape even more tempting. Scrolling pauses the thinking. It delays the choosing. It softens moments that feel too uncomfortable to sit with. And yet, the chaos it claims to soothe often grows louder beneath the surface.

Awareness does not mean rejecting technology or forcing distance. It means noticing how the phone is being used. Whether it's there to rest, to distract, to numb, or to disappear for a moment. In a decade already defined by transition and instability, attention becomes one of the few things that can still be gently reclaimed. Not perfectly. Not all at once. Just enough to stay present in your own life.

THOUGHTS RUNNING FREE

Sometimes I refresh again and again, not even knowing what I am searching for. Just waiting for something, but what?

Over time, scrolling becomes a distraction, a form of comparison, and a mild form of ignorance. Algorithms reinforce what we already think, conversations shrink to emojis, responses become memes "busted", and our attention becomes so fragmented that we forget how to perceive each other truly.

Sometimes I promise myself I'll check one thing, and two hours later, I am reading about topics that don't even interest me. It's not about the content, it's about the pull. Even conscious scrolling is tiring. Scrolling numbs boredom and reinforces comparisons.

The cycle stays predictable: **refresh, compare, forget, repeat.**

RELATABLE MOMENTS

You're sitting on the bus, wanting to relax, but you end up opening Instagram.
You pop home 'just for a minute' and lose half an hour.
You search for a recipe and end up watching three videos on a random topic.
You check your notifications before bed and then wonder why it's suddenly 1 a.m.
You try to concentrate, but your phone lights up again.

PAUSE & THINK

If attention is a currency, who or what benefits from yours?

What would fill your life if your attention were focused on yourself again instead of on a feed?

THE WORLD SCREAMS. MY HEAD ECHOES LOUDER. IF I AM CRAZY, IS IT ME, OR IS IT ALL OF US TRYING TO STAY HUMAN IN A WORLD THAT NEVER STOPS?

HOW DOOMED IS YOUR SCROLLING?

After scrolling online, I usually feel:

a) Energised and inspired, I love seeing what others create.
B) A mix of emotions inspired, but sometimes drained.
C) A bit worse. Comparison sneaks in without me noticing.

When I look back at my digital past, I mostly feel:

a) Nostalgic, those memories are part of my story.
b) Mixed. I have changed so much since then.
c) Embarrassed, I do not even recog nise that person anymore.

When I pick up my phone, it's usually because:

a) I am taking a break and want to relax.
b) I am bored or avoiding something.
c) I do not even know, it's just a habit.

When I post something, I:

a) Forget about it right after it's just for fun.
b) Check back a few times, curious about reactions.
c) Overthink it. I worry about what people will think.

If I took a week off social media, I would:

a) Miss the memes and updates, but I would be fine.
b) Feel disconnected at first, then relieved.
c) Feel lost, it's my main link to the world.

RESULTS

Mostly A's — *The Balanced Observer*

You have built a mindful relationship with social media. It's a reactive tool, not a control mechanism, keep using it with intention.

Mostly B's — *The Thoughtful Scroller*

You are aware of how it shapes your mood, but it still gets to you sometimes. A digital detox could help you reset your energy and rediscover inspiration offline.

Mostly C's — *The Emotional Mirror*

Social media feels heavy because it mirrors what you are working through internally. Try replacing screen time with journaling or in-person connection for a week and notice what changes.

HOW TO SLOWLY REGAIN YOUR ATTENTION

No detox. No shame. Just small decisions.

1. **Delay the first scroll of the day.** Just two minutes of silence before opening your phone will reset your pace.
2. **Name your reason.** Before opening an app, ask yourself: Am I bored, anxious, avoiding something, or am I actually interested? Naming it breaks the automatic cycle.
3. **Create a phone-free pocket.** A meal, a walk, a shower, choose a moment when your body is in charge instead of your screen.
4. **Create physical distance.** Leaving your phone at the other end of the room immediately reduces reflexive scrolling.
5. **Choose an exchange.** Replace a scrolling session with something that grounds you: stretching, journaling, breathing, or going outside.

You don't have to change your entire relationship with your phone in one day. Just choose a moment, a pause, when you look up instead of down.

> TEN MINUTES. AN HOUR. A WHOLE NIGHT GONE. DID I CHOOSE THIS, OR DID MY PHONE CHOOSE FOR ME? AND MAYBE THAT IS WHERE THE REAL DANGER LIES WHEN THE SCREEN BECOMES LOUDER THAN SILENCE. WE SCROLL INSTEAD OF FEELING, REACT INSTEAD OF LISTENING, AND SOMEWHERE BETWEEN NOTIFICATIONS AND NOISE, WE FORGET HOW TO SIT WITH ONE ANOTHER, ANOTHER PERSON, OR EVEN OURSELVES.

RANDOM BUT — WHAT ARE WE EVEN DOING WITH SOCIAL MEDIA?

THE OTHER DAY, MY PHONE SENT ME A NOTIFICATION: 11,334 photos saved on Snapchat since July 2014.

Eleven thousand fragments of life stored somewhere safer than memory. Screenshots of conversations that once felt urgent, blurry nights out, random selfies I don't even remember taking. The app knows more about my own memories than I do. A few minutes later, TikTok showed me how to download my entire Snapchat history.

Coincidence? Probably not.

Creepy? Definitely.

It made me pause: how long are we planning to keep all this? Will these accounts outlive us as digital museums filled with half-funny jokes and forgotten faces? Or will we ever delete them, the way we let go of old phone numbers or broken friendships?

Snapchat is still one of my most-used apps, but I cannot decide if keeping eleven years of photos is iconic or just excessive. Maybe it is both. Perhaps it is my own digital diary, a time capsule that remembers everything, even the things I have forgotten. Being twenty-something means living in this tension. On one hand, there is nostalgia. Those saved photos feel like proof of who I was.

On the other hand, there is anxiety. A reminder of how much time has changed, but I still feel stagnant, trying to figure out who I am or who I am supposed to be. How much of myself have I already given away to platforms that will outlast me? I keep asking myself: Are we capturing the moment, or are we trying to capture the moment? Are we living it or just collecting proof that it happened? The question is not whether we will keep or delete social media, but whether we have learned how to exist beyond it.

THOUGHTS RUNNING FREE

11,344 photos. Every version of me saved, uploaded, forgotten. Maybe that is what growing up online means: Learning when to remember and when to let go.

We do not just outgrow clothes, cities, or people, we outgrow digital selves, too. Old versions of us still live online, untouched, while we keep moving, or not. Maybe one day we will delete them. Or maybe we will not. Somewhere between keeping everything and letting go, we are all just figuring out what actually matters enough to keep.

When did you last add someone on Snapchat? How often do you even use it now? It used to feel like a universal tool for connection. Now, for many, it's faded into nostalgia, replaced by DMs, group chats, or voice notes that vanish as quickly as they appear. Maybe communication has not died. Perhaps it just evolved.

PAUSE & THINK

If you downloaded your entire social media history, what story would it tell about you? Would you keep it, edit it, or erase it?

How much of your life exists only online?

If social media disappeared tomorrow, which moments would you actually want to remember?

HOW ATTACHED ARE YOU TO YOUR DIGITAL PAST?

When your phone reminds you how many photos are saved:

(a) Panic time to delete.
(b) Shrug, it is a diary, who cares?
(c) Laugh, iconic, keep everything.

How often do you clear out your accounts?

(a) Monthly or yearly, I like a clean slate.
(b) Rarely, what is the point?
(c) Only if someone forces me.

How do you feel when looking at old posts?

(a) Embarrassed, who was that person?
(b) Nostalgic, it's all part of my story.
(c) Amused, it's a time capsule, nothing more.

RESULTS

Mostly A's — *The Curator*
Edits, prunes, and protects context, values a clean archive.

Mostly B's — *The Archivist*
Keeps the long view, sees feeds as living diaries.

Mostly C's — *The Time-Capsular*
Embraces the mess, treats platforms as museums of past selves.

Tie — *You blend modes*
Choose one small action this week: delete ten items, tag ten memories, or caption ten photos with what they taught you. This will show you how far you have come and help you learn to appreciate every part of your past.

COMMUNICATION BREAKDOWN

THE QUIET COLLAPSE OF CONVERSATIONS

FROM DIGITAL NOISE TO HUMAN SILENCE, communication has not disappeared, it has only changed form. We talk more than ever, yet listen less. Our phones stay within reach, but attention drifts elsewhere. Messages shorten, replies slow, and meaning blurs through screens. Somewhere between instant replies and ghosted conversations, connection became both easier and harder at once. This shift collides directly with the instability of being twenty-something, a decade already shaped by uncertainty, self-doubt, and emotional overload. When life feels unsettled, communication becomes lighter, faster, and safer on the surface, but thinner underneath. Convenience replaces depth. Control replaces presence.

Voice notes replace real voices. Emojis stand in for emotion. Entire relationships unfold through pixels. Somewhere between typing bubbles and seen at 2:04 p.m., something fundamental shifted. Talking became typing. Listening became scrolling. Moments that once held silence and eye contact now fill with screens and distraction. In the twenties, when identities are still forming, and emotions often feel too big to explain, the phone offers control over timing, tone, and distance. It allows responses to be delayed, edited, and softened. But it also removes the messiness where real connection lives.

We type "*How are you?*" without waiting for the answer. The pauses, hesitations, and tones that reveal how someone actually feels rarely survive translation into text. I am fine becomes a survival phrase, a verbal shield raised when explaining feels too exhausting. Messages are still unanswered, not out of cruelty, but out of overload. Communication becomes efficient, fast, and forgettable. The deeper layers slip away somewhere between notifications and distraction. The more updates are shared, the less understood people often feel.

This erosion of presence shows up in ordinary moments. A colleague asks a serious question, but the gaze drifts toward a screen mid-answer. The conversation ends before it begins. What once felt like human contact turns into background noise. *The question arises: is this disinterest, or has pausing long enough to listen become unfamiliar?*

Beyond work, the shift extends into public spaces. Buses, cafés, and waiting rooms carry a silence that did not exist before. Where conversations once sparked between strangers, heads now tilt downward in unison. Thumbs scroll. Retreat replaces curiosity. Isolation is not chosen, it happens automatically.

THOUGHTS RUNNING FREE

I sit with friends, and everyone is on their phone. I wonder whether to break the silence or if silence has become normal.

Children learn to swipe before they learn to observe or speak. Friendships, dates, and family moments unfold in partial presence, with one person speaking and the other nodding while checking notifications. Even with friends, there is often a silent choreography: one scrolls, another nods, both half-present. Phone calls feel intrusive. Ringing the doorbell got replaced by "I am here." Meeting in person feels like an effort. Presence now requires intention.

Post-pandemic life amplified this shift. We learned how to talk through pixels but forgot how to sit in the same room without needing a buffer. Vulnerability feels safer at a distance. Some things no longer fit neatly into text boxes. Some truths need space, silence, or shared air, things the internet cannot hold. This is not a failure of communication. It's a reflection of a generation navigating growth in a hyperconnected world. Being twenty-something already means balancing becoming and belonging, independence and insecurity. When everything feels transitional, depth can feel risky. Distance feels manageable. The quiet collapse is not the loss of words, but the loss of listening. Connection still requires presence, pauses, and the willingness to sit with discomfort. The challenge of being a twenty-something is not learning how to speak more but relearning how to stay.

PAUSE & THINK

When was the last time someone really listened to you without checking their phone, without rushing the silence?

When did silence last feel comfortable instead of awkward?

Who do you truly listen to, and who listens to you?

HOW DO I ACTUALLY COMMUNICATE BEST?

Rate each statement from 0 (never) to 3 (often):

1. I rehearse what I'll say instead of saying it.

(Never) 0 — 1 — 2 — 3 (Often)

2. I prefer texting to calling, even for emotional topics.

(Never) 0 — 1 — 2 — 3 (Often)

3. I avoid silence by filling it with words or distractions.

(Never) 0 — 1 — 2 — 3 (Often)

4. I multitask while talking, scrolling, cooking, and thinking ahead.

(Never) 0 — 1 — 2 — 3 (Often)

5. I notice when people's energy shifts while speaking.

(Never) 0 — 1 — 2 — 3 (Often)

6. I feel anxious if a message stays unread for too long.

(Never) 0 — 1 — 2 — 3 (Often)

SCORE REFLECTION

0–5 The Present Listener

You value connection and stay aware of tone, space, and emotion.

6–10 The Careful Communicator

You try to connect, but often overthink how you'll be received.

11–15 The Digital Reflex

You communicate quickly but feel less fulfilled. Try slowing down one call, one pause, one eye-to-eye talk at a time.

WHAT CAN YOU DO WITH THIS INSIGHT?

A quiz is only helpful if it helps you understand your behaviour patterns. Once you have recognised how you communicate, the next step is to decide what you want to do with this information. Here you can find out what the individual score ranges mean for your next step:

If you are a Present listener (0–5):
Use your strength. Your next step is to protect your presence, not just offer it. Set boundaries around screen time when you are with people you love. Encourage deeper conversations. You are the one who can bring connection back into the room.

If you are a cautious communicator (6–10):
Your next step is courage in small doses. Practise a moment of honesty every day:

- Say "I feel..." instead of making hints.
- Call someone instead of texting.
- Let silence be silence.

You don't have to fix conversations. Just approach them with less preparation and more honesty.

If you are a Digital Reflex (11–15):
Your next step is to slow down your response pace. Choose a conversation where you are fully present today, without multitasking, without scrolling, without typing while doing three other things. Consciously pause before you respond. Ask a more profound question. Presence grows minute by minute.

THE EYE CONTACT EXERCISE

Find someone you trust.

Sit across from them in silence for one minute. No phones, no distractions, no filler words, just eyes and breath.

Notice what surfaces: tension, warmth, awkwardness.

That minute says everything about how comfortable you are with presence.

What to do after the exercise:

Write down a word that describes how the silence felt. If it was uncomfortable, practise again. If it was calming, offer this presence to someone else. If it evoked emotions, ask yourself what your body was trying to tell you. Silence is feedback. Listen to it.

I REHEARSE MESSAGES LIKE TINY PERFORMANCES.
BUT SOMETIMES THE HARDEST LINE TO SAY IS:
WHAT I FEEL IS …

BOOMERLAND

LYING IN BED WITH MY GOOD FRIEND GIGI, WHO I MET on the island, I had one of those realisations that only arrive late at night, half-laughing, half-thinking: we've completely commercialised the word meaning the generation, boomer. It has such a strong presence in our generation that every time I use it or hear someone else say it, I can't help but giggle.

Gigi and I are two very different beings. She once accidentally ordered a suitcase online and was genuinely shocked at how fast it arrived. So shocked, in fact, that when she had already left the island, I was the one returning it for her. A very boomer situation, if you ask me. But then again, I catch myself too. There are moments when I do something and immediately think, wow, that was such a boomer move, like on New Year's Eve, filming the Harbour Bridge fireworks.

I zoomed in and out like there was no tomorrow, as if my phone wasn't already more than capable. Watching it back later was hilarious. Very earnest. Very unfiltered. Very boomer energy. And the funny thing is, it's never meant seriously. It's affectionate. It's playful. It's a way of laughing at ourselves when we realise we're not as effortlessly cool or digitally fluent as we think we are. It's the moment you notice yourself doing something slightly outdated, slightly chaotic, and instead of cringing, you laugh.

Do you ever catch yourself, or your friends, acting like a boomer for a second? And do you end up giggling about it, too?

Maybe Boomerland isn't an age or a generation. Perhaps it's just a moment.

II

MEETING YOURSELF

Where identity, age,
and self-image collide.

THE MYTH OF AGE

THIS CHAPTER FEELS BOTH CHALLENGING AND exciting to write, because age is never as simple as the number on an ID card. When I was younger, people often told me I had an "old soul," that I was unusually wise or mature for my age.

Was I really?

Back then, I rationalised it away: I spent time with older friends, played soccer with kids a few years older than me, started school early, and later repeated a class. Those things made me feel older than I was, although, looking back, I never truly was.

"*Feeling older*" did not make me any older, it just meant I was living through different events. Biological age is precise. It's tied to a birthday, a number, a candle, a light box, a tick. Lived age is elastic. It stretches with responsibility, snaps back with joy, and keeps shifting with context. Some days, we feel decades older. On others, we slip back into something almost childlike. We use age to judge: who dresses "appropriately," who we befriend, which choices are "right for this stage of life."

But in real life, the idea of age collapses the moment you actually look at people instead of numbers. Living in a coastal hostel for two months showed me how flimsy the concept of age really is. One night, a fellow traveller laughed and called me a "bubba" because he refused to believe I was 27 – until I pulled out my ID. Whenever I asked people to guess my age, they almost always said under 25. It felt strange and flattering at the same time. Here I was, with two degrees, years of travel, and time living in Sweden behind me, and still, people did not believe I was in my late twenties.

On the flip side, I have also heard people say 27 is "old," and I catch myself wondering: *Since when? Are we now the age we once thought was ancient at parties? Did the tables turn and we are the ones saying, "this generation..."*?

The longer I stayed in the hostel, the clearer it became, that once you strip away the numbers, what matters is how people show up in their energy, their curiosity, their values. Similarly, friendship adds another layer as two of my closest hostel friends, Kim and Euan, were 19 years old. I did not choose them because of their age, I chose them because our values aligned like going on fishing trips, late-night talks about life and philosophy, laughter that had nothing to do with numbers. At the same hostel, friendships stretched from 18 into "no number needed."

I even told Kim that if we had met back in Europe, I might not have hung out with him, not because of his age, but because our lives there would not have aligned. Different routines, different cities, different circles. That is the point: age is not the story. Timing is. That awareness carries both gratitude and urgency, a quiet understanding that not all connections are meant to last forever, but some are meant to happen exactly once.

Therefore, being twenty-something often means meeting people in between versions of yourself. Before careers harden, before routines settle, before life becomes too fixed to overlap easily. Timing feels fragile in these years, and that fragility creates rare alignments. Friendships form not because they are convenient, but because, for a brief moment, lives are open enough to meet. People meet when they are meant to meet, not when their birth years line up neatly. Either way, there is still this strange cultural obsession with asking, "*So, how old are you?*". Sometimes it's curiosity. Sometimes context. Sometimes control. Younger people ask it more, we did too. I still ask sometimes, partly out of habit and partly because at work I legally have to check IDs if someone looks under 25 here in Queensland. But outside of those moments,

I wonder what we are really trying to measure: years or energy?

Once, during the island's annual race week, an internationally attended sailing event that transforms the otherwise quiet island into a high-profile social hub filled with yacht crews, sponsors, and affluent visitors, several older men (in their fifties) invited us onto their boat for lay day. They joked, "*Why spend your day off with us old lads?*" I said, "*Because I like to hear your stories and learn from your experiences.*" I have always been drawn to older people hearing their stories, their perspectives, their quiet wisdom, their joy when someone genuinely listens. You can learn from any age group, but specific lessons arrive only through time. Maybe that is why I feel so at home in mixed-age groups: There is less pressure to perform a life stage and more space to be a person.

In my twenties, that relief feels radical. So much of this decade is shaped by invisible deadlines: careers, relationships, achievements we think we should already have. Being in mixed-age spaces dissolves that pressure. There is no checklist to perform, no comparison to win, just the quiet permission to exist without proving where you are supposed to be by now.

One morning, I woke up to a text from Georgia, my induction buddy on the island, the person I arrived with and immediately clicked with, asking if I wanted to join her for a beginner yoga class. Georgia loves the outdoors, hiking, yoga, and long conversations, and she became one of those grounding presences you find in new places when everything still feels unfamiliar. Not to forget, I was exhausted from work, but something in me pushed to go. That is where I met André who joined me for yoga instead of Georgia, my Brazilian god, as I like to call him. After class, we went for coffee, ran into Georgia, and ended up at the wildlife park for a coffee and a stroll. Over lattes and conversations about work and life, André said something that stuck with me: "*I feel like I need to settle down now – career, stability, my biological clock is ticking.*" It sounded like something people warn you about in your twenties, as if urgency has an expiration date attached to age. Without thinking, I laughed and said: "*Hold on, I am almost ten years younger than you – and I feel the same way.*"

That moment crystallised it for me. The urgency we feel for security, stability, change, freedom which doesn't follow a neat timeline. It does not wait for a specific birthday. It arrives when it arrives, whether you are 19, 29 or 39. Maybe that is the real myth: that age is supposed to dictate where we should be. What actually pushes us forward is not the number, but the feeling of "*I cannot stay like this anymore.*"

THOUGHTS RUNNING FREE

Jamie laughs and calls me "Bubba." I show my ID: 27. He still squints. Some people say I do not look a day over 23, a compliment and a mismatch. Then someone else says, "Late twenties? Old." Too young for some, too old for others. So, which is it? Maybe neither. Maybe both. Maybe age is not the number at all, but the number of moments you are in.

So, what is age, really? In the end, age feels less like a fixed number and more like a shifting lens. People can look 21 and feel 35 or look 35 and feel 21. To judge life stages, friendships, or opportunities by a number feels limiting, when what really matters is: How do we connect in a given moment? How honest we are with ourselves. How we respond to the urgencies inside us.

Being twenty-something is not about being behind or ahead. It's about learning to recognise when a feeling is asking for change, and trusting that timing is allowed to look different for everyone. Biological age is a construct. Timing is a teacher. Give yourself grace.

PAUSE & THINK

Think of a moment when you felt "younger" than your age and one when you felt "older." What caused the difference – people, place, or timing?

Have you been told you "Look younger" or " older"? How did it land?

Where in your life do you still let a number limit you?

SOME SAY I LOOK 21. OTHERS CALL 27 "OLD." MAYBE AGE IS JUST A COSTUME, AND TIMING WRITES THE SCRIPT. WHAT COUNTS IS NOT THE NUMBER OF YEARS, BUT HOW WE ANSWER THE MOMENT WE ARE IN.

HOW OLD ARE YOU REALLY?

Not your ID card – your felt age. Emotional, physical, social, and inner.

Tally
A = 1
B = 2
C = 3
D = 4

A free Saturday looks like...

A) Sleep in, brunch, scroll, or game
B) Adventure/day trip / explore
C) Errands, meal prep, organise
D) Book, tea, early night

Travel style:

A) Hostels and spontaneity
B) Road trip with friends
C) Boutique hotel, culture, wine
D) Slow travel, wellness, retreat

In a group of strangers, you...

A) Jump right in
B) Observe, then join
C) Prefer 1:1 conversation
D) Connect deeply with just one or two people

Conversations that light you up:

A) Jokes, memes, gossip
B) Dreams, adventures, "what ifs."
C) Plans, careers, relationships
D) Meaning, purpose, the universe

Friendships tend to form...

A) Mostly with people my age
B) Through shared experiences
C) Across ages if values align
D) Mostly with "older souls."

Relationships feel best when...

A) Fun, light, experimental
B) Balanced – freedom + effort
C) Stable and values-aligned
D) Purposeful, deeply intentional

First morning thought:

A) "Five more minutes..."
B) "Where's my coffee?"
C) "What is on my to-do list?"
D) A quick gratitude or intention check-in

When someone asks your age, you...

A) Laugh – feels irrelevant
B) Answer proudly – just a number
C) Answer, then reflect on how different you feel inside
D) Use it as a check-in about where you have been

Birthdays feel...

A) Party hard, celebrate big
B) Experience > gifts (trip, concert, dinner)
C) Dinner with close friends
D) "Just another day" with a quiet reflection

When someone guesses your age, you feel...

A) Flattered if they say younger
B) Confused – it changes constantly
C) Unbothered – it is not the point
D) Reflective about perception vs. reality

RESULTS

Add up your points (10–40) or notice which letter you chose most often.

Mostly 1s – The Playful Spirit (Emotional Age ~18–23)
Curious, spontaneous, and light-hearted. You chase experiences, follow sparks, and keep things open. You are still exploring who you are and that is exactly right for now.

Mostly 2s – The Explorer (Emotional Age ~24–30)
You are walking the bridge between exploration and responsibility. Some days you want chaos, some days calm. You are actively shaping your life, even if it does not look "sorted" from the outside.

Mostly 3s – The Grounded Builder (Emotional Age ~31–40)
You crave stability, alignment, and long-term foundations. You still enjoy fun and spontaneity, but meaning, health, and future-you have a more decisive vote now.

Mostly 4s – The Old Soul (Emotional Age 40+)
Perspective and presence guide you. You value depth over drama, quality over noise, honesty over performance. You have lived enough to know what matters and you protect it.

Mixed answers?
You have range. Different contexts unlock different ages, playful at brunch, old soul at 2 a.m., kitchen talks. That flexibility is a strength, not a problem.

I DON'T KNOW WHAT CRISIS I AM GOING THROUGH

BEING TWENTY-SOMETHING FEELS LIKE MOVING from one mini-crisis to the next. Not dramatic enough to call it a breakdown, but intense enough to question everything. Sometimes they are not even real crises, just a buildup of tiny things that suddenly make you ask:

Who am I becoming? What am I even doing?

The strange part is how ordinary days hold these quiet disruptions. A simple conversation can spiral into an existential crisis. Like when my best friend Cosma called and said, "*We should run the half-marathon in Mainz next year.*" Meaning the Marathon in mid-2026. It sounded innocent enough until I realised what she was really asking: *When will you come home*? I could not answer. Because "*home*" stopped being a location a long time ago. It became a feeling I keep chasing through places, people, and choices. Maybe this is the twenty-something condition: constantly balancing what you want, what others expect, and what reality actually gives. It's like carrying a backpack full of invisible things: doubts, hopes, comparisons. Some days it feels heavy. Other days, it feels like everyone else's backpack is lighter.

The older I get, the more I see that most of us are just unpacking our own layers, one decision, one heartbreak, one spontaneous plan at a time. Every new challenge feels like a test of identity: *Am I still the same person, or did I just grow again without noticing?*

THOUGHTS RUNNING FREE

Today I panicked because my friend ran a half-marathon

and I couldn't, and I could not decide what to eat for dinner. Tomorrow, I will convince myself to move to another country. Next week, I will call it personal growth. Maybe the point is not to stop having crises but to realise they are not crises at all. They are just check-ins with yourself.

Practical choices collide with emotional ones. Deciding whether to extend a visa, stay in a job, or move cities is not just about logistics, it's about identity, belonging, and who we are becoming in the process. When my two cats, who had been living with my ex for the past two years, almost came back to me, it felt symbolic. As if I were regaining a part of myself that I hadn't known I had given away. And then there are the conversations that shift everything. During Race Week on the Island, I had conversation with men twice my age, successful, calm, grounded. Listening to their stories was humbling because they weren't chasing certainty anymore. They were living proof that life does not need to be figured out to be meaningful. It made me wonder: Maybe what we call a crisis is just another word for growth.

PAUSE & THINK

What if there is no single "crisis" at all, just layers of becoming?

Which part of your current uncertainty could actually be a sign of growth?

What are you learning from what feels uncomfortable right now?

WHAT IS IN YOUR BACKPACK TODAY?

Pick three you are carrying right now:

☐ Visa/location anxiety

☐ Money guilt ("I should have saved more")

☐ Friend-milestone envy

☐ Family expectation

☐ "Am I wasting time?"

☐ Relationship confusion

☐ "Should I move back home?"

☐ "Everyone else has a plan."

☐ Just want to rest

Look at the three you ticked. Which one feels heaviest, and which one could you put down, even just for today?

JOURNAL REFLECTION

Over time, I realised my "crises" were not chaos, they were communication. Every overthinking moment was my mind trying to show me something I had not yet faced. Now I try to listen before spiralling. Because once you understand what your feelings are trying to tell you, you stop fearing them.

THE FINANCIAL ANXIETY NO ONE TALKS ABOUT

MONEY IS ONE OF THE LOUDEST ANXIETIES OF OUR twenties, yet everyone whispers about it like it's a shameful secret. People say, "*follow your dreams*," but dreams cost money. People say, "*Travel while you are young*," but flights aren't free. People say, "*save for the future*," but the present already feels expensive.

Most of us grew up believing adulthood meant stability. Instead, we got rising rent, unpredictable jobs, and the feeling that everyone else is financially ahead, buying homes, securing promotions, building lives with timelines that look nothing like ours. Also, money is not just numbers, it's safety, freedom, belonging, and identity. Sometimes financial fear shows up as guilt: "*I should have saved more*" or "*I shouldn't have bought this*" even though you were excited to buy it. Often, it is as a comparison, "*They are the same age, and look how far ahead they are.*" Sometimes, as shame, "*I am still figuring it out when everyone else seems secure.*"

THOUGHTS RUNNING FREE

Maybe I am not behind. Maybe I am building slowly.
Stability can grow from chaos, not all at once.

I realised that travelling teaches money in its own language. One month, you are eating pasta from a $1 packet, trying to survive. The next time you are in a scenic flight over the Whitsundays, where life feels like art. Money becomes something elastic, stretching, tightening and surprising. It shows us how quickly it goes and how resilient we become.

Your twenties are financially contradictory: You are told to "enjoy life" and "be responsible" at the same time. You are asked to build a future while barely understanding the present. But here is something I have learned: *Feeling behind financially does not mean you are doing life wrong. It means you are human.* It means you are learning how to build stability in a world where stability is rare. Money fear is not weakness. It's your nervous system trying to protect you. And with time, you learn to separate: Your worth from your wallet, your identity from your income, your future from a number on a screen.

PAUSE & THINK

What emotion hides underneath your money stress, fear, shame, comparison, or pressure?

What belief about money did you inherit that no longer fits you?

What would "financial safety" feel like, emotionally, not numerically?

> MONEY MEASURES MOMENTS, NOT WORTH. YOU ARE ALLOWED TO BUILD A LIFE AT YOUR OWN PACE.

WAVES OF HOME

LIVING AWAY FROM HOME OR MOVING AWAY FOR THE first time is a surreal experience because it brings up every emotion at once. Homesickness does not always mean missing a place because often, it's the longing for belonging. I left home for the first time at sixteen for an exchange year across the world in Australia. Later, I lived with my ex-partner in a different city, studied in Sweden, and travelled across countries again. Each move carried its own lesson, but the same truth remained: *once you leave home, in whatever form, the experience never stops shaping you.*

There are moments when homesickness doesn't even feel like sadness, but rather like a pain without a clear cause, as if I am homesick for something I cannot name. Sometimes I miss a smell, a tone of voice, a certain quietness that once felt ordinary. Other times, I realise I am not longing for a specific place at all, but for a version of myself that existed there.

Last year in Brisbane, after four months of travelling, one of those waves hit me hard. I sat by the Brisbane River and called my friend Trevor, who was halfway around the world but awake while Europe slept. My working holiday visa still hadn't been approved while I was stranded in Australia (it could be worse, I know), but my money was running out, and even though Ariah, Hayden and Juhnaya in had generously taken me in, I felt unattached. That afternoon, I booked a flight home. I needed it not because Australia had failed me, but because sometimes the heart needs to return to something familiar, even briefly, to remember its rhythm. Homesickness comes in waves. It does not mean failure, it means the heart still reaches for warmth, even when the body has learned to be independent. Maybe belonging is not something you find once. Perhaps it's something you keep learning how to carry.

The older I get, the more I understand that freedom has its own kind of nostalgia. Leaving home was never about running away, it was about curiosity, ambition, and becoming myself. But every flight I have taken, every apartment I have packed up, carried a slight echo of loss. I am old enough to leave and make decisions, to build a life somewhere new. But still young enough to miss it all: the smell of coffee in my mother's kitchen, the sound of my brother's laugh, the sense that someone always knows where I am.

THOUGHTS RUNNING FREE

Sometimes I wonder if I am homesick for people, for places, or for a version of myself I left behind. Maybe belonging is not fixed, perhaps it's something we carry. Leaving does not mean forgetting. Distance does not mean indifference. Sometimes choosing yourself is the most loving thing you can do.

Being twenty-something means living in this contradiction, learning independence while quietly missing the simplicity of being known without needing to explain. Sometimes growing up feels like building new homes while mourning the old ones that shaped us.

One evening, I asked my roomie Jeanine, "*Do you ever feel disconnected from home?*" She smiled and said, "*I grew up in Dublin, but I was never a city girl. Ireland never felt like home.*" Her words stayed with me. Finding a home away from home. You can feel far from everything familiar, family, language, and landscapes, and still try to create a version of home somewhere else. Maybe that is what your twenties are really about: *not searching for one perfect place but learning to feel at home in many.*

The guilt of staying away is real. And it is not just about people who travel, it's about anyone who leaves, some move for work, for studies, for partners, or simply for a new beginning. Leaving always carries a quiet ache, the sense that by choosing yourself, you might be abandoning someone else. We live in a world that tells us to chase opportunity, yet when we do, we feel guilty for it.

We are privileged to go, and yet we still feel bad about it. Maybe it is because generations before us didn't get the chance to, or because social media glorifies distance as freedom. But leaving does not always feel free. It often feels heavy. No one wants to be called selfish for following their own path, yet choosing yourself can look like betrayal to those who stay. The truth is, everyone's parents, friends, and colleagues act from their own needs, fears, and hopes, not out of disinterest, but out of being human. That is the hard truth of adulthood: everyone carries their own reasons for staying and their own reasons for going.

PAUSE & THINK

Homesickness can feel heavy, but it's also proof of connection. It shows that love, bonds, and memories root so profoundly that they can't be missed.

> HOME IS NOT A SINGLE PLACE. IT IS THE PEOPLE, THE MEMORIES, AND THE QUIET RITUALS THAT REMIND YOU WHO YOU ARE, NO MATTER WHERE YOU LAND.

REFLECT

What do I miss most when I feel homesick:
People, places, routines, or moments?

Have I ever booked a ticket, made a call,
or acted different because of this feeling?

When did guilt last mix with gratitude about
where I am now?

How do I define "home" right now by
geography or belonging?

CARRY YOUR HOME

Write down three things that make you feel at home:
a meal, a song, a smell, or a ritual.

____

____

____

Then ask: How can I bring one of these into my current life, wherever I am?

Home does not always mean where you started.
Sometimes it is something you learn to build again and again.

PARENTS AS PEOPLE

I HAD JUST HUNG UP THE PHONE WITH MY MOM when a strange silence filled the room. Not the kind of silence that feels empty, but the kind that makes you realise how much has changed without you noticing, like growing close but also growing apart. There are so many things that have shifted over the past few years. Part of me feels far away, not only in distance, but in thought. I do wonder: *Do you ever feel that, too? Has your relationship with your parents changed in quiet, almost invisible ways?*

My mum and I used to be inseparable. She was my closest confidant, my daily call, my automatic comfort. But somewhere between growing up, moving away, and learning independence, that bond stretched thin. It is not gone, simply different. Conversations now sound more like updates than long talks. What used to be "Tell me everything" sometimes becomes "Just give me the summary." Love remains, but silence has grown between the lines. Maybe this is what happens when you start building a life of your own. The roles shift. The child who once needed guidance becomes the one explaining, reassuring, translating her own world back to them. It is strange, this quiet reversal of care. Sometimes I miss the version of us that laughed at the most minor things. I miss being understood without having to explain myself. And yet, I know that growing apart does not mean losing love, it means learning to love differently, from new distances.

There also arrives a moment when parents stop being just "parents" and start becoming people. Not heroes. Not villains. Just humans who did their best with what they knew at given time, like everybody else. The illusion fades quietly. You begin to see their fears, their insecurities, their past regrets. You realise they had whole lives before you existed, dreams they might have paused, sacrifices they never mentioned, parts of themselves that never came back.

THOUGHTS RUNNING FREE

I used to tell my parents everything. Now I edit parts out not out of secrecy, but out of space. They were once my entire world. Now we stand on different continents, still bound by the same gravity. Maybe love just changes its distance, but never its pull.

I started to notice it in the small things. The hesitation in my mum's voice when she asked if I was happy. The way my dad sometimes stayed silent when I talked about staying abroad, as if he wanted to say stay but knew he could not. They both wanted me to go further than they ever could, but they also missed the version of me that was still close enough to call from the next room. Distance is not just measured in kilometres. It's emotional, too. There is the guilt of being away, a guilt that stretches across borders. It's not just for travellers or expats. It's for anyone who is ever left: for a job, a degree, a relationship, or simply the need to grow. The guilt whispers: *You chose to go, even when leaving was the only way to become who you needed to be.*

And yet, my parents once did the same. They made choices that took them away from their own families, their own dreams, their own versions of home. That could be the cycle we all leave in separate ways, and each generation learns to forgive the other for it. The truth is, everyone acts from their own level of awareness. People can only meet you as deeply as they have met themselves. And that includes also our parents.

Sometimes they cannot fully understand the lives we are

building, not because they do not care, but because they have never experienced or walked this kind of freedom. We are privileged to go to study abroad, to work overseas, to choose our paths, and privilege always comes with the echo of guilt. Regardless, understanding changes everything. The shift from childhood to adulthood changes your perspective entirely. Once you stop expecting perfection, the resentment softens. The arguments become less about right and wrong and more about wanting to be seen. You start forgiving your parents for being human, for saying the wrong thing, for worrying too much, for loving imperfectly. There is a strange peace in that acceptance. Love remains, even as the form changes. They were once my entire world. Now we orbit each other with different lives, same pull. Maybe the twenties spent growing up, do not mean breaking away, perhaps they mean learning how to love from a distance.

PAUSE & THINK

(When) Did your relationship with your parents last change, and how did it change?

Was it a conversation, a silence, or simply time passing?

When did you first realise your parents were human?

What part of their story do you understand differently now?

What truth about you do you wish they could see?

FRIENDSHIP WITHOUT PROOF

THE OTHER DAY, MY FRIEND JUHNAYA CALLED ME while she was sitting with her sister, Charlotte. Mid-conversation, Charlotte asked her something simple but unexpectedly heavy: "*How do you know if someone is one of your good friends, or just one of many?*" That question stayed with me long after the call ended. Because the truth is, it is hard to answer. Not because the answer does not exist, but because real friendship rarely fits into measurable categories. There is no clear line, no checklist, no ranking system. Friendship, at least for me, is not something that needs constant confirmation. I know someone is my friend when I do not have to question it.

We do not need to speak every day. We do not need constant updates or proof of closeness. What matters is knowing that I can call her, ask how she is really doing, and trust that we are there for each other when it matters. Friendship is not measured in proximity for me, but in effort and care. In the quiet certainty that the connection holds, even when life gets loud or distant. I told Charlotte exactly that. And I also told her that it was a valid question to ask. Because somewhere along the way, friendship started to feel like something that needed to be counted. Who talks most. Who shows up most. Who texts first. Who sees whom the most. But some of the deepest friendships I have exist outside of daily contact. There are people I have not seen in years, yet I know I would always be welcome at their dinner table. No explanation needed.

Juhnaya added something that made me smile. She said some friends are like seasons. That felt familiar. I have used that metaphor myself, without realising how true it still is. Some friendships walk with you through entire chapters. Others arrive for a moment, teach you something essential, and then quietly step aside. That does not make them less real. It makes them honest.

THOUGHTS RUNNING FREE

There is no "better" answer. Different friendships serve different roles. What matters is recognising which ones nourish you, and which ones you have outgrown.

Friendship is not measured in time, distance, or frequency. It is measured in safety. In showing up without being asked. In knowing you can disappear for a while and still return without having to explain who you became in the meantime. Maybe the real marker of friendship is not how often someone is present, but how present they are when they are. This was not about closeness. It was about recognising who stays without asking

---

PAUSE & THINK

Who are the people you feel safe not talking to for a while?

Who can you call without rehearsing what you will say first?

Which friendships feel steady, even when life pulls you in different directions?

THE FRIENDSHIP CHECK-IN

Answer honestly. There are no right outcomes.

When life gets heavy, who do you think of first?

a) Someone you talk to daily
b) Someone you trust deeply, even if you rarely speak
c) Someone who once mattered, but feels distant now

A real friendship, to you, feels like:

a) Constant communication
b) Mutual effort without pressure
c) Unspoken understanding

When you reconnect after time apart, the feeling is usually:

a) Awkward, like catching up with a stranger
b) Familiar, like no time passed
c) Warm, but clearly changed

FRIENDSHIP DOES NOT NEED PROOF. IT DOES NOT NEED DAILY PRESENCE OR CONSTANT REASSURANCE. IT NEEDS TRUST, KINDNESS, AND THE FREEDOM TO GROW WITHOUT BEING ABANDONED. SOME FRIENDS STAY FOR LIFE. SOME STAY FOR A SEASON. BOTH CAN SHAPE YOU DEEPLY.

WHEN WE OUTGROW EACH OTHER

GROWING UP MEANS LOSING PEOPLE YOU THOUGHT would stay forever. No one warns you that some of the deepest heartbreaks of your twenties will not come from lovers, but they will come from friends. Friendship grief is quiet. It does not get break-up songs or comforting clichés. It happens slowly: fewer messages, shorter calls, plans that never come to fruition. One day, you realise you have not spoken in months, but you still remember their favourite coffee order or their favourite song.

Distance is not always measured in kilometres. Sometimes it's measured in effort.

I also used to think friendships were supposed to last forever in an ideal world. But now I know they last for the season they are meant to be in, for who you were when you met, for what you needed at the time, for the version of you that existed then. Because after all our growth creates gaps in different values, different timelines, different emotional depths.

THOUGHTS RUNNING FREE

I do not miss the friendship we had. I miss the version of me you knew. Maybe letting go is not forgetting, maybe it's honouring the chapter for what it was.

Some friends stay on the ride. Some get off at earlier stops. Part of growing up is grieving the ones who helped build you, even when the story ends without a fight, without a villain, without a moment you can point to and say, "*This is where we broke.*"

Sometimes two people simply grow in different directions,

very parallel for a long time, then suddenly not. It hurts in a way language struggles to hold. Because it's losing a history, not just a person, it's losing a witness to your becoming. But friendship grief also taught me something essential: **Connection does not need permanence to matter. Some friends were meant to shape a chapter, not the whole book**. And the ones who stay across continents, time zones, and quiet stretches, they remain because the connection grows with you, not against you.

PAUSE & THINK

Which friendship are you still grieving?

What did it give you, and what did it teach you?

Who grows with you now, not away from you?

> SOME FRIENDSHIPS END WITHOUT BREAKING. THEY SIMPLY STOP FITTING THE PERSON YOU ARE BECOMING, AND THAT IS A QUIET KIND OF COURAGE.

III

NOISE, ANXIETY, AND THE MIRROR

When the world becomes too loud,
the mind has nowhere to hide.

WHEN LIFE GETS TOO LOUD

THERE ARE DAYS WHEN THE WORLD FEELS unbearably loud, not just through sound, but through pressure. The noises hide everywhere: in expectations, notifications, and opinions that arrive before you even ask for them. Sometimes it's not the world that is loud, it is life itself: every thought, every plan, every what-if competing for space in your head. Closing the bar at night has become one of those rare moments of truth. The second the music cuts off, silence pours in like a wave. What is left is not peace but exhaustion that had been hiding under the noise all along. The twenty-somethings have been full of lessons disguised as chaos. I learned that love is not supposed to sound like confusion. That wanting someone who cannot meet you, there is nothing romantic about it, it's exhausting. And that sometimes, the most significant relief is when your heart finally stops arguing with your mind.

But also, with that being said, even airports feel different now. Standing in line, surrounded by movement and chatter, an unexpected wave of anxiety hits. Years ago, when I worked as a flight attendant, flying felt routine. Now, on the other side of the check-in counter, the thought of leaving the ground presses down like an invisible wall. Fear rarely asks permission before arriving. And for a long time, I mistook overthinking for awareness. I thought if I could feel through everything, every text, every silence, every almost, I'd find peace. Instead, it became its own kind of chaos. There were nights I lay awake replaying moments, conversations, things I could not change. I kept blaming it on people, on timing, on love until I realised most of the noise was mine. It was the sound of me trying to control what simply needed to be accepted.

Then, somewhere between exhaustion and clarity, something shifted. I stopped overthinking not because I mastered control, but because I stopped betraying myself. When you act from your own values, there is nothing left to doubt. Once you honestly think, not spiral but think, you stop overthinking, because when actions align with morals, there is peace. When you tell the truth, even when it hurts, you do not have to replay the story later. Maybe that is what healing actually sounds like: not silence, but inner steadiness.

THOUGHTS RUNNING FREE

Sometimes peace does not come when everything's calm. It comes when you stop negotiating with what you already know. The world hasn't gotten quieter, I just started listening to myself.

The kind of quiet that comes when you stop chasing closure and start trusting your own choices. There is a version of me that used to panic about everything needing to be controlled, fixed, and understood. But lately, I have felt something new: a calm detachment, the kind that says, "*I do not give a fuck*," not out of coldness, but out of peace.

Me, not caring is not the absence of feeling, it's my freedom of knowing what deserves my energy. Silence, stillness, even a single breath, they do not escape, they are reminders. Not everything needs a reaction. Not everyone deserves an explanation. Peace is not the absence of noise, it is hearing yourself again beneath it. But the noise is not just outside. At some point, it moved in. That is where self-perception, and the way my brain learned to scan for danger, really began.

Before moving on, pause here. This section is not about fixing the noise but noticing how you survive it.

PAUSE & THINK

What part of your inner noise is not yours to carry anymore?

When was the last time your thoughts were louder than your truth?

Can you tell the difference between reflection and rumination?

And when did you last mistake noise for connection?

BEING QUIET DOES NOT MEAN BEING WEAK. SOMETIMES SILENCE IS THE LOUDEST FORM OF SELF-RESPECT.

REALITY CHECK

When Life Gets Too Loud

How do you usually respond when the world overwhelms you?

a) Turn up distractions: Scrolling, music, noise, constant motion.
b) Shut down and avoid everyone: Close the door, go quiet, disappear for a bit.
c) Find one quiet ritual: Breathing, walking, journaling, grounding.
d) Push through until you crash

RESULTS

A — *The Numb-Outer*
Your instinct is to outrun the noise by creating more noise. It's a form of self-protection, not avoidance. Your work is not to remove distraction, it's to learn what happens when you slow down.

B — *The Disappearing Act*
You retreat to survive. Silence feels safer than vulnerability. Your work is learning how to stay connected without feeling exposed.

C — *The Quiet Regulator*
You have begun to build internal coping skills. Not perfectly, but honestly. Your work is trusting that these small rituals count as emotional maturity.

D — *The Over-Performer*
You push past your limits until the body intervenes. This pattern often forms in people who learned early on that rest must be earned. Your work is allowing for a pause without guilt and recognising the signs earlier.

MINI INSIGHT

None of these responses means that something is "wrong." They reveal how you have survived so far. The goal is not to fix the pattern but to recognise it so that you can choose a softer one next time.

TRIGGER LIST

WHAT SETS YOU OFF (AND WHY IT MATTERS)

WE ALL HAVE TRIGGER MOMENTS THAT MAKE OUR hearts race faster than they should. A tone. A look. A silence. What feels immediate often is not. That familiarity is not always danger, sometimes it is the echo of a younger version of you asking to be heard. The part that learned early on that silence often meant something was wrong. When I started doing the work, I realised how much of my reactivity made sense once I traced it back. Silence used to trigger me deeply. Not getting a text back. A missed call. Someone going quiet mid-conversation. A pause that lasted too long. It was never just about the moment itself. It was about the person I once was the one who felt left out, the one who was not chosen, the one who learned to be strong in order to survive. It was not about them. It was about my history.

Being twenty-something during COVID-19 shaped that history in ways I did not fully understand at the time. Surrounded by uncertainty, isolation, and constant disruption, my anxiety learned to rely on reassurance to feel safe. Silence became a threat. A pause felt like abandonment. My nervous system adapted by staying alert, always scanning for signs that something might go wrong. So even now, when someone goes quiet, my first instinct is to panic. My mind jumps ahead, inventing scenarios, building stories, spiralling into assumptions. But now, something else happens too. I pause. I breathe. I ask myself, “Is this about today, or is this about back then?” Most of the time, it is back then. Over time, I stopped seeing triggers as flaws. For a long time, I believed being triggered meant being dramatic or weak. Now I understand it differently. A trigger is data. It is information from the past that still wants to be seen. It is my body saying, "Something here feels familiar."

Silence is not the only trigger. Overstimulation plays a role as well. Loud places. Crowded rooms. Airports. Closing the bar late at night. I get overwhelmed quickly, not because something is wrong with me, but because my system still remembers what it felt like to be constantly on alert. During COVID-19, my nervous system was trained to look for danger everywhere. That training does not disappear just because circumstances improve. Even now, I can be in the safest place and still feel unsafe. That does not make me fragile. It makes me human.

THOUGHTS RUNNING FREE

My triggers may not be flaws. They are directions, pointing me toward the parts of myself that still need softness. Not everyone who touches your wound means to hurt you. Sometimes they are just holding the same place where they were once broken.

Rejection carries its own weight too. A shift in tone. A change in energy. Someone forgetting to include me. Things that might roll off someone else's back can sit heavy on mine. When I feel rejected, even briefly, it touches older wounds: wanting approval, wanting to be loved, wanting to be chosen. And honestly, that is not something to be ashamed of. We all want to be chosen.

One of my deepest triggers is losing control. Not knowing the plan. Not knowing what someone feels. Not knowing when something will happen. Uncertainty used to terrify me. I believed that if I could control everything in terms of my emotions, my decisions, the people around me, then nothing could hurt me. But trying to control everything became the thing that hurt the most.

Now, when uncertainty arises, I try to meet it with curiosity instead of fear. Understanding triggers is not about avoiding life or preventing discomfort. It is about knowing yourself well enough that your reactions no longer run the show. It is not about blaming others for how you feel. It is about listening to what your reactions are trying to tell you. Sometimes a reaction is a warning. Sometimes it is a reminder. Sometimes it is simply a version of you that needs reassurance. When silence hits now, or when overstimulation creeps in, I remind myself of something simple: **peace is also a response**. Triggers do not define who you are. They reveal where you are healing. This was never just about the noise. It was about learning where my body learned fear. Take a moment before answering the questions. Triggers often make more sense when you approach them with curiosity instead of judgment.

PAUSE & THINK

What reaction feels bigger than the situation?

What memory might that reaction belong to?

What would your younger self need to hear in that moment?

THE TRIGGER TRACE

Pick one trigger and trace it back:

1. THE TRIGGER

What happened?

2. THE REACTION

What did you feel in your body?

3. THE STORY

What did you assume or fear?

4. THE ORIGIN

When did you first feel something similar?

5. THE REFRAME

What is a kinder interpretation today?

SELF & PERCEPTION

THE SPACE BETWEEN HOW I SEEM AND HOW I FEEL

WHERE IT STARTED: THE PANDEMIC YEARS

During the COVID-19 pandemic, life shrank into a small, tight space. Everything familiar changed shape. Days blended into each other. Silence grew louder. Anxiety became a shadow that followed me into places it had never lived before, especially inside my own head. That period rewired my emotional system. I became hyper-aware, hyper-reflective, sensitive to every shift in mood. Every feeling felt like a signal. Every quiet moment felt suspicious. The body learned vigilance before the mind learned language. When the world reopened, my nervous system didn't. It stayed cautious, scanning, evaluating, asking: "Is this safe? Am I okay? What am I feeling?". The body doesn't always cooperate with logic. Sometimes it reacts before understanding. Sometimes it remembers without explaining.

This chapter comes from that space, not fear, but honesty.

There is a strange tension in being twenty-something: the pressure to appear confident while quietly doubting how others see you. Outwardly, composure performs itself well. Calm. Helpful. Reflective. Loving. Inwardly, uncertainty hums, asking questions that rarely make it to the surface.

My friend Tess once asked me, "What guiding principles are you telling yourself daily?". It caught me off guard. She told me she asked because I seemed grounded. Bubbly. Kind. As if I had things figured out. What she didn't know was that the night before, I had gone to bed overwhelmed by sadness and anxiety about the past, so heavy it almost pulled me under. What she saw was the outside. What I lived with was the inside. I told her the truth I could name in that moment: that I remind myself to be kind, to be grateful, and to trust that things will work out. And that is true. Those are the principles I live by. But they are not effortless truths. They are reminders. Anchors. Things I repeat because without them, my mind spirals. The gap between how I appear and how I feel is not dishonesty. It is protection.

Growing up, I learned early how to figure things out on my own. I was the child people didn't worry about. The capable one. The self-sufficient one. Over time, which became an identity. So now, even when I struggle, I often carry it quietly. Not because I don't need support, but because I don't want to hand the weight of my worries to someone else. That isolation doesn't always look dramatic. Sometimes it just looks like strength. This is where self-perception or self and perception begins to blur.

THOUGHTS RUNNING FREE

Sometimes I wonder why the same type of situation finds me again. Do I attract it or am I still learning how to meet myself differently?

In crowded spaces like trains, airports, waiting rooms, my body tightens. Logic tells me nothing is wrong, yet my nervous system braces for danger. Anxiety rehearses worst-case scenarios until they feel real. The mind knows it's safe. The body doesn't listen. That mismatch is exhausting. It's one of the hidden realities of my twenties: learning to carry invisible tension while performing stability. No one posts it. Almost everyone feels it. The task isn't to erase these reactions. It's to meet them honestly, to recognise that the outside world and the inside world don't always move at the same pace. Self-perception isn't just about how you see yourself. It's about how you think you're supposed to be seen. And sometimes, the greatest exhaustion comes from maintaining the distance between those two.

Read the questions slowly. There is no correct response, only honest ones. Being twenty-something often comes with pressure and doubt.

PAUSE & THINK

What parts of yourself feel visible to others and which remain hidden?

Where do you spend energy appearing "collected" instead of allowing yourself to be real?

What does your nervous system need that your self-perception doesn't allow you to ask for?

YOUR TURN

FEAR MAPPING

Write one recurring fear. Trace it back: is it learned, situational, or inherited?

SELF-DIALOGUE

Let your critical voice speak. Then answer it from a place of compassion, not correction.

PAST REFLECTION

Choose a memory that shaped a fear you still carry. What did it teach you and what can you release?

JOURNAL

What would it look like to be honest without having to be strong?

FACING FEAR ISN'T ABOUT ERASING IT. IT'S ABOUT RECOGNISING WHERE IT LIVES, WHY IT LEARNED TO PROTECT YOU, AND CHOOSING GENTLY TO KEEP MOVING ANYWAY.

HOW DO I FEEL?

THERE ARE DAYS WHEN THE MOST CHALLENGING question is not "*What do I want?*" or "*Where am I going?*" It is something much simpler, much more complicated: **How do I actually feel?**

I never realised how difficult that question was until my twenties started stretching me in all directions. One moment I feel grounded, the next untethered. I walk back into work after a long break, and I catch myself thinking: *Am I sad? Am I happy? Am I overwhelmed? Am I fine?* Sometimes the emotions arrive all at once, and sometimes nothing arrives at all. It's strange to live inside your own body and still struggle to read it. The confusion is not dramatic. It is subtle. It is waking up with a heaviness you cannot name. It is feeling restless in the middle of a calm moment. It is crying out of nowhere and not knowing whether it is relief or exhaustion. It is sitting at work, smiling, while something in your chest keeps asking: **Are you okay?**

For a long time, I thought something was wrong with me. But the truth is, this confusion did not appear out of nowhere. It has roots, long ones. The truth is: **emotional clarity is a skill.** No one teaches you how to read your own inner weather. We are taught how to work, how to study, how to be productive, but not how to sit with ourselves and ask: *What is the temperature inside me right now?* Sometimes I feel two things at once. Or nothing at all. Sometimes happiness comes with a faint ache in the background. Sometimes sadness sits next to joy, like roommates. It is not madness. It is humanity, the in-between feelings. People assume emotions follow clean labels: **happy, sad, stressed, and excited.**

But most twenty-somethings live in the in-between, where everything overlaps.

You Can Feel:
Proud and Uncertain
Excited and Scared
Grateful and Overwhelmed
Lonely and Independent
Tired and Hopeful

You can miss people you do not want back. You can love your life and still feel lost in it. People can surround you and still feel like you are floating slightly above yourself. None of it means you are broken. It means you are paying attention. But also, the reason it's so hard to answer, "*How do I feel?*" is because we are often asking the wrong person: *our self-perception, the internal mirror that has been shaped by childhood, expectations, anxiety, social media, and a thousand invisible pressures.* My self-perception during the pandemic became distorted. It made me believe every uncomfortable feeling was a crisis. That every slight shift meant something was wrong. That if I did not feel good, I was failing.

This chapter exists because untangling that takes time and language. Naming the confusion does not solve it, but it softens it. And maybe for someone reading this, the softness is enough.

This is not a test. It is a check-in with yourself, exactly as you are today.

THOUGHTS RUNNING FREE

I may not need to sort every feeling into a drawer. Perhaps some emotions are meant to be held, not understood. Maybe the question is not "How do I feel?" Possibly it is, "Can I sit with myself long enough to find out?"

LEARNING TO CHECK IN

When I feel confused now, I ask smaller questions:

- Am I physically tired or emotionally drained?
- Am I overstimulated or underwhelmed?
- Am I anxious, or am I anticipating something?
- Am I sad, or am I in transition?
- Am I lonely, or do I just need rest?

Not all feelings need answers. But they do need acknowledgement. The point is not to feel good all the time. The real work is learning to feel honestly. Without rushing. Without labelling everything as a problem. Without assuming that uncertainty equals danger. Some days, I know exactly how I feel. Other days, I have no idea, and that's okay. Being confused does not mean being lost. It means you are still learning the language of yourself.

PAUSE & THINK

What feeling do you misinterpret most often: sadness, stress, boredom, or loneliness?

Where in your body do you feel emotion first?

What emotion is most complicated for you to name honestly?

YOU ARE NOT DIFFICULT. YOU ARE NOT DRAMATIC. YOU ARE NOT BROKEN. YOU ARE JUST LEARNING TO READ THE WEATHER INSIDE YOURSELF, AND THAT TAKES TIME.

WHEN FEELING EVERYTHING DOESN'T MEAN YOU'RE BROKEN

FOR A LONG TIME, I WONDERED IF THERE WAS something wrong with me. *How can someone read emotions so well and yet feel so overwhelmed by them?*

I notice my feelings early on. Sometimes even before they surface, I can sense when I am about to cry, and yet I can't let myself. Once, I said to my mum, "*So that you know, I am about to cry. Don't be surprised.*" She asked, "*Would you like a hug?*" And I said, "*Not yet. I'll let you know when I am ready.*"

That moment stuck with me because it says a lot about how my emotions work. I am aware of my feelings. I just have to control how and when I show them to others. For a long time, I thought this made me cold, dramatic, or difficult. Now I understand **it's just my nervous system demanding space**. Emotional intelligence is often equated with constant composure, constant self-control, and "*good handling of feelings.*" But some of the most emotionally intelligent people I know feel everything too strongly, too quickly, and too intensely. They can:

- Sense a change in a room within seconds.
- Read a face, tone of voice, or pause before anyone else notices.
- Predict long in advance when something is going to hurt.

The problem is not that they don't understand emotions. The problem is that the body reacts faster than it can regulate itself. This is how I feel it: **my mind understands. My body overheats.** Sometimes emotions manifest as warmth, pressure, or a tingling under my skin. I know exactly what's happening, but I can't always let it out on command. Crying doesn't always come when it "*should.*" Words don't always fit into a short text message. I need time. I need distance. I need control over the contact. Not because I don't want support, but because I need to calm my system down before I let someone get close to me.

GROWING UP AS A SENSITIVE PERSON IN A WORLD THAT IS TOO LOUD

LOOKING BACK, THE SIGNS WERE ALWAYS THERE. AS a child, I loved being alone in my room and losing myself in my imagination. I could focus on creative things or random topics for hours. Control always gave me a sense of security: **plans, routines, knowing what was going to happen next**. My body has always been picky. I still pay far too much attention to how a fork feels in my hand, the thickness of the handle, the spacing between the prongs, the weight. There are some clothes I cannot wear because the fabric feels wrong against my skin. Sand on my body when I try to apply sunscreen? No. Sand on my feet, and then walking on specific stones that make that scratching noise? No way.

Noise quickly overwhelms me. When too many conversations are happening at once, my brain tries to listen to all of them and fails at every single one. In noisy rooms, I get overstimulated, not because I am shy, but because my senses have no filter. My brain hears everything. My body feels everything. And at some point, it just shuts down. From the outside, this can seem like moodiness, aloofness, "*too sensitive,*" or "*too much.*" From the inside, it feels like my system is running at maximum volume, without a volume control.

MY DAD'S MEMORIES

I DID NOT ALWAYS LOOK OVERWHELMED. I OFTEN looked quiet, but quiet did not mean harmless. Quiet sometimes meant I had found something to disappear into. I could keep myself busy for hours, peeling wallpaper, painting, focusing so profoundly that the world around me became background noise. I did not need much external entertainment. I needed a corner where nothing changed too quickly.

There is a story my dad tells that still makes me laugh because it captures my brain perfectly. We were at the Edersee (a lake close to our home, where we used to have family holidays). He was fishing. I stood behind him, unusually calm, unusually silent. He turned around and asked why. I had eaten the bait, including the maggots. His question was rational. My answer was not. "*It is food, isn't it?*". Even as a child, I moved through the world literally. Sensory first. Logic second.

Overwhelm did not always come from sadness. It came from too much, too many inputs, too many responsibilities at once, too many moving parts. I remember phases where small things spiralled because I could not organise them inside my head yet. Even animals could feel like too much. We had hamsters, and I was overwhelmed by them. Not because I did not care, but because caring came with noise in my nervous system: guilt, pressure, responsibility, the fear of doing it wrong. When something depended on me, my system either went into control mode or shutdown mode, there was rarely a calm middle ground.

Loudness was always the quickest switch. If a room got too loud, my body reacted before my mind could explain it. I did not debate whether it bothered me. I felt it in my skin. As a child, I learned fast where calm lived. I looked for the quieter presence. I looked for the place where my nervous system could soften again. Sometimes I did not need advice. I needed a low voice, a safe silence, a moment of being held back into regulation. That is the complicated part of being "sensitive." It looks emotional from the outside, but it is often physical. Volume does not just annoy me. It destabilises me. **And because the world rarely adjusts its volume for anyone, I adjusted instead.** I became good at leaving rooms. I became good at retreating. I became good at being fine. I learned how to look normal while feeling like everything inside me was too much.

WHAT IT LOOKS LIKE IN MY TWENTIES

CHILDHOOD GAVE SENSITIVITY MORE PROTECTION. A bedroom door could solve a lot. A predictable routine could reset my nervous system. Someone else made the plans. Someone else set the pace. In my twenties, sensitivity becomes harder because adulthood removes the buffers.

Now, sensitivity shows up in places that do not allow pauses. In restaurants during rush hour. In staff rooms. In airports. In an open-plan living. In friendships where everyone talks at once, I try to listen to everyone and end up hearing none of it correctly in relationships where conflict feels like volume, even when no one raises their voice. In my twenties, I plan my energy the way other people plan their weekends. I chose seats near the exits. I scan for noise before I scan for faces. I need recovery time after social time when being with the wrong crowd. I crave structure, not because I am boring, but because structure lowers the risk of overwhelm. I do not chase control because I want power. I chase control because it creates a sense of safety.

This is also the decade where sensitivity meets expectation. The world assumes adulthood comes with thicker skin. People call it "*coping*." People call it "*being easy-going*." People call it "*not making a big deal*." But a sensitive nervous system does not become less sensitive just because the calendar says so. The difference is that, as an adult, I have to carry it myself. I have to build my own quiet. I have to choose my own boundaries. I have to become the one who protects me.

THOUGHTS RUNNING FREE

Maybe nothing is wrong here. Maybe your system just runs louder, faster, and deeper than most. Maybe the reason it feels exhausting is not because your emotions are too much, but because the world rarely pauses long enough to meet them. If your emotions sometimes arrive without language, that does not mean confusion. It means your body speaks first. And maybe needing time, space, or silence has never been avoidance. Maybe it has always been self-respect.

Sometimes it still looks like withdrawal. Sometimes it seems like an organisation. Sometimes it looks like leaving early. Sometimes it looks like needing silence after work, even when nothing "bad" happened. Sensitivity is not only a reaction to a crisis. It is a reaction to accumulation. And the older I get, the more precise the truth becomes: **sensitivity is not something to outgrow**. It is something to understand. Something to translate into adulthood. Something to stop apologising for.

PAUSE & THINK

When does your emotional intensity signal information rather than dysfunction?

Which situations activate your nervous system before conscious thoughts intervene?

Which of your behaviours currently serve to regulate rather than avoid?

NERVOUS SYSTEM MAPPING

1. NOTICE THE MOMENT

Think of a recent situation where emotions felt overwhelming, even if nothing "*bad*" happened.

2. NAME THE FIRST SIGNAL

What showed up first: pressure, warmth, tightness, tingling, restlessness, or the urge to withdraw?

3. ASK THE GENTLE QUESTION

Instead of asking "*What is wrong with me?*" ask: "*What is my system asking for right now?*"

4. TRANSLATE, DON'T JUDGE

Finish this sentence in writing or quietly in your head: "*This reaction makes sense because I needed* ____."

HOW SENSITIVITY SHOWS UP NOW

Which sentence feels most familiar?

A. You often know something will hurt long before it actually does.

B. You feel emotions clearly but need time before sharing them.

C. Noise, chaos, or tension drain energy faster than people realise.

D. Control, structure, or exits help you stay regulated and present.

REFLECTION

Whichever option fits most often does not describe a flaw. It describes how care already happens behind the scenes.

IF YOU FEEL EVERYTHING QUICKLY AND DEEPLY, THAT DOES NOT MEAN YOU ARE BROKEN. IT MEANS YOUR NERVOUS SYSTEM NOTICES MORE BEFORE IT CAN PROTECT YOU. NOTHING HERE NEEDS FIXING. IT NEEDS PACING.

HOW I ACTUALLY REGULATE MYSELF

EVEN IF IT LOOKS LIKE AVOIDANCE

OVER THE YEARS, I HAVE DEVELOPED MY OWN RULES for managing my emotions:

I often need distance first, then connection later. I want hugs and closeness, but on my own terms My own autonomy". My system calms down faster when I choose the moment myself.

I use familiar stimuli to regulate myself: series I already know, podcasts I've already heard, familiar voices, and stories. This isn't laziness, it's my brain preferring predictable sounds to new stimulation.

I alternate between intense concentration and complete confusion.

I can write an entire book draft in two months and then have difficulty responding to simple messages. This is not a discipline problem, but an energy problem.

I have a quick, erratic mind. I change topics quickly, connect ideas that seem random from the outside, and get frustrated when others can't follow the leaps my brain makes automatically. For a long time, I judged myself for this.

Now I see it differently: this is not a failure. It is a system. A nervous system that: *perceives early, feels deeply, regulates best when it is autonomous*. It's not that I can't deal with emotions. I just can't always deal with them at the drop of a hat. Sit with these questions gently. They are meant to create space, not pressure.

PAUSE & THINK

Do your emotions come faster than your reactions?

Do you sometimes know exactly what you are feeling but are unable to show it?

Do you need space before you need comfort, even from people you love?

If so, chances are you are perfectly fine. Your nervous system simply works on a different schedule.

SMALL TIPS FOR REGULATION
(that do not affect your sensitivity)

THESE ARE NOT SOLUTIONS. JUST GENTLE AIDS. NAME it early on. Think of them as options you can return to when things feel overwhelming.

"*I feel like I am about to cry. I just need a little time first.*" - Naming it takes away your shame and gives you the ability to act. Choose the right moment.

Tell others: "*I want to talk about this, but not now. I'll come back to it when I've calmed down.*" This is not avoidance, but self-respect.

Reduce one level of sensory overload. Noise, light, touch, tasks, choose one thing you can reduce: *a quiet room, dimmed lights, fewer conversations, fewer open tabs.*

Use familiar comforts. Watch a programme again, listen to a podcast again, paint, doodle, move slowly. Predictable stimulation = less work for your brain.

Let your body catch up. Sometimes emotions want to come out later: through tears in the shower, while writing in your diary in the evening, or through conversations days after the event. Feelings expressed later are still valid feelings.

THE MIRROR LIES

THE MIRROR HAS NEVER BEEN JUST GLASS. IT REFLECTS more than a face, it also carries everything that has been projected onto it over time: expectations, comparisons, and quiet judgment. In the age of social media, which mirror no longer exists in one place. It multiplies into screens, lenses, and curated feeds. Every swipe offers a new reference point: sharper jawlines, smoother skin, leaner bodies.

Maybe this sounds familiar: I take ten photos, delete them all, and still, none feel like me or do me justice. The problem isn't the camera. What sits underneath this frustration is not vanity. It is the search for recognition. Perhaps it is how I see myself or what I expect to see. Sometimes I stare into the mirror and wonder if my body still recognises me. Maybe it is waiting not for perfection, but for peace.

The search is less about capturing the perfect image and more about seeking proof of existence, proof that identity can be seen, validated, and remembered. Body image becomes a negotiation between how one feels inside and how others are assumed to perceive them. Travel, relationships, and even small conversations reveal how differently people project their identities onto others.

A compliment that feels dismissive. A tagged photo that feels unflattering. The silence of no likes at all. Each becomes a mirror of its own.

Social media magnifies this tension by archiving everything, turning fleeting self-doubt into a permanent record. What once lived only in the bathroom mirror now lives in the cloud. This pressure does not stay abstract. It shows up in ordinary moments.

At work one day, two girls ordered vodka, lime cordial, and water "*because it has fewer calories.*" I told them, "*You do not need it.*" One smiled, surprised, and said quietly, "*It is just what society makes us do.*" Her words lingered.

Earlier that same day, I had told my friends Evie and Sofia that I was finally losing weight. Evie looked at me, puzzled. "I did not know you were trying," she said. I had been, but slowly, without pressure. Healing takes time. After the pandemic, it felt more complex than ever to feel comfortable in my own skin. I refused to stress my body into change. Those conversations made me realise something: **healing transforms the body from within**. When the mind softens, the body follows. Once the body feels safe, it gives back its changes naturally and without force. The process is not about becoming smaller or fitting an image. It is about becoming at peace with existing as you are. *This is where the mirror begins to lose its authority.* The quiet truth is that the mirror cannot define you. Age, identity, and body image are always moving. Experience carves maturity into gestures, resilience into posture, and stories into scars. A tired face can hold resilience. A scar can mean survival.

THOUGHTS RUNNING FREE

I try on jeans that fit from last year, but they're too tight. The mirror says one thing. My body says another. Some days I love the reflection. Some days, I pick it apart until nothing feels enough. Is it my body that changed, or the way I look at it?

The body is often treated as a public project open to commentary, comparison, and measurement. Social media amplifies that exposure by placing images side by side, encouraging constant judgment. What once existed as a fleeting thought in the mirror now becomes a permanent digital archive.

The body becomes not only lived but performed.

The paradox is this: when the mirror is taken as absolute truth, the individual loses the narrative. When the body is understood as a companion in growth, the reflection becomes only one part of a much larger whole. This was not about the reflection. It was about reclaiming the story behind it.

Before answering the questions, notice your first reaction. It often tells the truth faster than your thoughts. This is not about fixing how you look. It is about noticing whose voice shapes the way you see yourself.

PAUSE & THINK

When was the last time you looked in the mirror and felt neutral, not hostile?

What if the goal were not to change the reflection but to understand the person inside it?

ASK YOURSELF

Whose standards shape my self-image most?

Which parts of myself do I celebrate, and which do I hide?

Do I feel more confident offline or online, and why?

If no one could see me online, how would I dress, pose, or carry myself differently?

THE MIRROR DOES NOT JUST SHOW SKIN. IT SHOWS MY DOUBTS, MY HUNGER, MY LONGING TO BE ENOUGH. SOME DAYS I TRUST IT. SOME DAYS I LOOK AWAY. BUT EVERY TIME, I COME BACK. AND EACH TIME, I GET TO DECIDE HOW MUCH AUTHORITY IT HOLDS.

IS THE MIRROR TALKING OR ME?

Looking in the mirror usually leads to:
a) Critiquing details immediately
b) A quick check, then moving on
c) Noticing strengths first

After scrolling online, I feel:
a) Worse than before
b) About the same, with slight doubts
c) Grounded in self-awareness

Compliments about appearance are:
a) Hard to believe
b) Nice, but not always trusted
c) Accepted with ease

The body feels most like:
a) An enemy to battle
b) A project to maintain
c) A partner to live with

RESULTS

Mostly A's — The mirror often speaks louder than your own voice. Self-perception is shaped primarily through external standards.

Mostly B's — Balance exists, but comparison still slips in during moments of exposure or fatigue.

Mostly C's — Self-image and lived experience align more often than not. Acceptance is present, even if it is not constant.

IDENTITY WHIPLASH

WHO AM I RIGHT NOW?

THERE ARE SEASONS OF LIFE WHERE IDENTITY FEELS like trying on coats in a department store. None of them quite fit, but you keep slipping in and out of versions of yourself, hoping one finally feels like home.

Being twenty-something means shifting identities faster than people can keep up with. One minute you are the friend who gives excellent advice. The next day, you are crying in the shower, wondering when your life will start to feel like yours again. Sometimes it feels like becoming a different person depending on the country you are in. Germany, Sweden, Australia. Each place unlocking a version of me that did not exist before. The strange part is how quickly it changes. You grow, then outgrow. You become someone, then let her go. **You reinvent, refine, release.**

THOUGHTS RUNNING FREE

Some days I feel brand-new. Other days, I feel like an echo of who I used to be. Maybe identity is not a destination. Maybe it is every version I have ever tried on.

It is emotional whiplash, a constant swivelling between who you were, who you are, and who you might become next. And half the time, the people around you still talk to the version of you they met days, weeks, months, or years ago. They don't realise how much can shift in the days, months, or silent seasons where you disappear to figure yourself out.

Identity is not a fixed point. It is a moving target. Sometimes you chase it. Sometimes it chases you. And sometimes it slips quietly through your fingers, leaving you to rebuild from scratch.

I used to think I needed a solid answer to "*Who am I?*". Now I think the braver question is: "*Who am I becoming?*", "*Do I like this version of me?*".

Because identity is not built through certainty, it is built through motion. Through leaving home. Through heartbreak. Through trying, failing, trying again. Through late-night conversations that undo you, and early-morning flights that reinvent you.

Identity expands in moments of stillness too. In those familiar yellow-bench pauses, where you are forced to sit with the person staring back at you and admit that you have changed again. Maybe the truth is this: you are not meant to be one thing. You are meant to be a series of becomings.

This chapter is not about knowing who you are. It is about noticing who you are becoming. You do not need to have the answer yet. These reflections are here to help you listen.

PAUSE & THINK

Which version of you feels most like home right now?

Who sees you as you are, not as you were?

If identity is fluid, what are you afraid of letting go?

> YOU ARE NOT LOST. YOU ARE BECOMING.
> IDENTITY IS NOT SLIPPING, IT IS SHIFTING
> INTO WHO YOU ARE MEANT TO BE NEXT.

IDENTITY SNAPSHOT

Right now

1. NAME THE VERSION (WITHOUT JUDGMENT)

Finish this sentence slowly, without explaining or correcting it:
Right now, I feel most like the version of myself who is

____.

There is no wrong answer. This is simply a snapshot, not a conclusion.

2. NOTICE THE NEED (NOT THE FIX)

Complete the sentence:
This version of me needs more ______________________
and less ______________________________.
This is not a plan. It is a signal.

3. WHAT NO LONGER FITS

Write down three things that belong to an older version of you. They might be roles, expectations, habits, or labels others still use for you.

______________ ______________ ______________

Nothing here has to be rejected forever.
You are only noticing what feels heavy right now.

4. RELEASE WITHOUT REPLACEMENT

Read this sentence slowly:
I do not need a final version of myself in order to move forward.
Pause after reading it.
Notice what reacts. That reaction is information.

HOW IDENTITY SHOWS UP RIGHT NOW

Choose what feels closest today, not always

When someone asks how you are, you usually feel:

a) Unsure how to answer
b) Like you're between explanations
c) Comfortable answering from where you are now

Looking back at past versions of yourself feels:

a) Disorienting or emotionally distant
b) Familiar, but no longer accurate
c) Like a foundation you have built from

Thinking about the future version of yourself feels:

a) Pressured and undefined
b) Possible, but unclear
c) Open rather than urgent

RESULTS

Mostly A's — You are in active transition. Identity feels unstable because it is rearranging, not because something is wrong.

Mostly B's — You are between versions. Old identities still echo, but they no longer get to decide for you.

Mostly C's — You are anchored in the present. Becoming feels integrated, even if it is still unfolding.

None of these states are permanent. None of them mean you are behind.

IV

LOVE, ALMOST-LOVE AND LETTING GO

Where the connection becomes
both the teacher and the test.

LOVE, ALMOST-LOVE, AND LETTING GO

LOVE IN YOUR TWENTIES FEELS A LOT LIKE WALKING through fog: you see outlines and catch glimpses, but the path never stays clear for long. It is excitement and confusion tangled together: **the almosts, the maybes, the not-quite-enoughs**.

I used to think love was about finding the right person at the right time. Now I know it is often about meeting the wrong person at the right time, someone who mirrors your hidden parts, challenges your patience, and forces you to grow in ways you did not plan. There was someone once. Someone magnetic is the kind of connection that pulls you before you can rationalise it. It was electric, impulsive, and honest.

For a moment, it felt like the universe had tilted slightly to make room for the possibility of us. But connection does not always equal compatibility. This kind of love, the intense, unfinished kind, has taught me more about myself than any calm, steady romance ever could. It shows you where you still ache to be chosen, where you confuse chaos for passion, and where you are still trying to heal the parts that feel unworthy of quiet love. When it ended, I did what most people do: searched for reasons, replayed words, read between lines that were already closed. I wanted answers. But sometimes there are none. Sometimes people do not choose you not because you are not enough, but because they do not know how to pick themselves.

THOUGHTS RUNNING FREE

Sometimes love does not stay. Some connections are not meant to stay. They arrive to show you what you tolerate, what you desire, and what you deserve next. Almost-love is not failure. It is information.

Over time, I learned that closure does not always come through conversations. Sometimes it arrives through silence, through time, through the small ways you start treating yourself better. There were days when I overthought every message, every pause, every "*what-if.*" But that overthinking eventually exhausted itself. Because when you start living in alignment with your own values, you stop needing explanations for why someone could not meet you there. When you stop betraying yourself to keep someone close, peace quietly replaces obsession.

Now, love looks different to me. It is not about intensity, it is about safety. It is not about chasing, it is about being met. It is not about fireworks, it is about steady warmth. I do not crave love that shakes me anymore. I crave love that stays. The kind that feels like home, not a test. And until that arrives, I am learning to give that same steadiness to myself.

PAUSE & THINK

What patterns keep repeating in your relationships, and what are they teaching you?

When was the last time you felt seen without needing to explain yourself?

What does "being ready" for love mean to you?

ALMOST-LOVE CHECK-IN
WHAT WAS IT REALLY ABOUT?

This is not about analysing the other person. It is about understanding what that connection activated in you.

1. Name The Almost (Without Romanticising It)

Finish this sentence honestly:
That connection felt intense because it gave me ______________.
Examples might be:

- attention
- distraction
- hope
- validation
- a sense of being chosen
- emotional familiarity

No answer here makes you weak. It makes you aware.

2. Separate Connection From Compatibility

Read each line and mark what felt true:

- I felt deeply drawn to them, but often emotionally unsettled.
- I confused intensity with closeness.
- I waited for consistency instead of receiving it.
- I explained away behaviour that hurt me.
- I felt chosen sometimes, but anxious most of the time.

You do not need to count. Notice which lines landed in your body.

3. What This Relationship Taught You (Not What It Failed To Be)

Complete one or more:
This connection showed me that I still ____________________.
This connection revealed where I need more ________________.
This connection clarified what I will no longer ______________.

Learning does not mean it was meant to last. It means it mattered.

4. Practising Closure Without Contact

Read this sentence slowly:
I do not need another explanation to choose peace.
Sit with it for a moment.
Notice whether relief or resistance shows up.
Both are information.

HOW YOU EXPERIENCE ALMOST-LOVE

Choose what feels closest most of the time, not always.

When a connection feels uncertain, you tend to:

a) Overthink every message and silence
b) Feel conflicted but try to stay grounded
c) Step back once patterns become clear

Love usually feels like:

a) Emotional highs and lows
b) A mix of comfort and confusion
c) Safety, steadiness, and mutual care

Letting go feels hardest because:

a) You want answers and clarity
b) You fear missing out on potential
c) You know peace requires distance

RESULTS (NON-JUGEMENTAL)

Mostly A's — You attach through intensity. Almost-love feels addictive because it mirrors unmet needs, not because you are too much.

Mostly B's — You are aware of patterns but still emotionally invested. Growth is already happening, even if it feels messy.

Mostly C's — You value emotional safety. Letting go hurts, but it does not destabilise you the way it once did.

None of these responses mean you loved wrong.
They reflect where you are learning to love yourself.

ALMOST-LOVE TEACHES YOU THE SHAPE OF WHAT YOU WILL NO LONGER ACCEPT. LETTING GO IS NOT LOSING LOVE. IT'S MAKING SPACE FOR ONE THAT DOES NOT REQUIRE YOU TO DISAPPEAR.

THE "WHAT-IFS"

MANY OF THE LOUDEST WHAT-IFS ARE NOT ABOUT choices or paths, but about people we almost chose and versions of love that almost stayed. The question of *what-if* captures attention and divides opinions. It lingers like an echo, always present yet never fully understood. The uncertainty lies in its origin: *does it come from the head or the stomach? Is it fear of leaving a comfort zone or the voice of rational caution?*

There is no scientific answer because what-ifs show up differently for everyone. For some, they appear in overthinking loops, a mind running endless scenarios. For others, they surface when reality collides with unfulfilled desires. My own what-ifs often arrive in mental spirals, building stories that exist only in my imagination. A guiding question I'll ask myself: "*What is the worst that could happen?*" And then: "*What is truly the worst that could happen?*"

But with that being said: This is not permission to break laws or be reckless. It's a reminder not to let unanswered what-ifs overshadow what is actually possible. Because the what-ifs go both ways: *What if I do not talk to this person? What if I do not go on this trip? What if I stay exactly where I am?* Funny how the negative what-ifs scream louder than the quiet ones full of possibility. In love, what-ifs linger differently.

What if I had stayed a little longer? What if I had spoken sooner? What if I had asked for less, or more?

Almost-love creates its own parallel timelines, ones that feel unfinished because they never fully lived in reality. These what-ifs are not signs of regret, they are signs of attachment searching for meaning.

Also, I do want to tell you that the inspiration for this chapter came from a conversation with my former roommate Jeanine. While we we're reflecting on her life, it became clear how much her what-ifs had shaped her path. Her situation was as followed: If she had stayed with her former partner, she might still be in the United States, and we never would have met. If she had stayed in her old job, she might never have moved to Australia in the first place. What I have realised is that small decisions can change entire timelines. Her what-ifs could have kept her stuck, but instead they became doors. In that way, the what-if becomes both a source of fear and a doorway to change. Uncertainty does not just threaten stability, it can also open unexpected opportunities. The same is true in love: some people leave so that a different version of you can arrive.

PAUSE & THINK

What are your personal what-ifs?

How have they shaped your path so far?

Do they still hold the same weight today?

Have they changed with age or experience?

Which what-if is attached to a person rather than a decision, and what would change if you released it?

HEAD VS. GUT

Sometimes the most challenging part is not the choice itself but figuring out which voice we are listening to.

HEAD SAYS	GUT SAYS
Gather data.	Notice energy.
Compare options.	Do I feel constricted
Reduce risk.	or expanded?

Both can be right.
The art is learning which one is speaking and which one you want to follow in this moment.

A TINY REFRAMING YOU CAN USE TODAY

If your what-if is fear-led:

What if I try, and it's uncomfortable... and I grow?

If your what-if is regret-led:

What if I do not try, and I keep wondering?

You do not have to fix your whole life. You need one honest experiment.

FROM WHAT IF → WHAT NOW

1. Write down one what if that is loud this week.
2. List the realistic worst case (1–3 lines, not a movie script).
3. List the most likely case (be honest, not dramatic).
4. Write the smallest next step you can take in the next 24 hours.
5. Schedule it. Do it.
6. Afterwards, debrief in three sentences:
    - *What actually happened?*
    - *How did it feel?*
    - *What did I learn about myself?*

This is not about being fearless. It's about proving to yourself that you can survive your own what-ifs.

YOUR PERSONAL WHAT-IFS

What are your top three what-ifs right now?

What have they done to you so far — protected, stalled, or redirected you?

Which "what- if" no longer belongs to you?

Which one still deserves a small experiment?

Have your what-ifs changed with age or experience?

WHAT-IFS ARE NOT THE ENEMY. IGNORING THEM IS. LISTEN, TEST, ADJUST, THEN TURN WHAT IF INTO WHAT NOW. SOMETIMES THE BRAVEST WHAT-NOW IS LETTING GO OF THE VERSION OF LOVE THAT ONLY EXISTED IN IMAGINATION.

MODERN DATING, EFFORT, AND EMOTIONAL HONESTY

AFTER LOVE COMES THE LEARNING CURVE OF MODERN dating, where clarity has to be relearned. We meet people who test our patience, our communication, and our boundaries until honesty becomes an act of self-respect rather than a strategy.

THE IN-BETWEEN

This is not a chapter about blaming genders. It is about the confusing space where modern dating exists, a world of apps, mixed signals, blurred intentions, and constant performance. It is about how exhausting it feels to want something real in a culture where attention is easy, but presence is rare.

I was with my ex-partner for almost eleven years. We started dating at the age of fourteen, which now feels impossibly young. We grew up together: as teenagers, as young adults, as two people trying to figure life out. There were heartbreaks, mistakes, and moments when love and pain blurred. People around us meant well, but often spoke too loudly. We learned, stumbled, and loved each other in all the wrong and right ways. Looking back, I am surprised we stayed together as long as we did. The person I am today would have left much sooner. Back then, we did not yet understand ourselves, our boundaries, or what love could mean beyond comfort. By twenty-five, when my mind caught up with my experiences, I realised something life-changing but straightforward: *the love I received was not the love I wanted*. Even if we had found a rhythm, it was no longer mine. So, I ended it. After we broke up, I went on what I now call side quests, meeting new people, dating lightly, laughing, feeling, disappearing again. There were kind males and good conversations, yet somehow, I always ended up choosing the familiarity of what I already knew. At the time, it felt inevitable. Now I see it was a cycle I had to live through to outgrow it finally.

When I moved to Sweden, I thought I was ready to start again. I was not. I downloaded Hinge for a week, deleted it, re-downloaded it months later, went on two polite dates, and then ghosted or got ghosted. Nothing stuck. After my not so successful dating life, came a crush that lasted half a year. He once said, half-joking while we were walking home from a party, "*I'd never date you.*"

That was it, the moment the crush lived up to its name. It crushed me. I did not even really know him, yet it hit deeply. Looking back, it was not about him at all. It was about me still learning what I was ready for and what I was not. But it also woke me up. I did not need validation. I needed healing. Healing took time. I had to grow in how I communicated, stop chasing unavailable energy, and stop romanticising almosts. Every misstep taught something new: *closure does not create peace, self-respect does.*

BOYS, GIRLS & MESSY CONNECTIONS

Modern dating feels like a paradox: everyone's available, yet connection feels rare. A conversation can start with a heart emoji and end in silence. Between the swipes, the waiting, and the unspoken "what are we," what people crave most is not attention, it is clarity. So many connections hover in limbo: not casual, not committed, just almost something. Everywhere, the same story echoes: "*We are seeing each other, but it's not exclusive.*"

Even tough three months later, it is still the same. It has become hard even to define what dating means anymore. It really makes me wonder: *How did something built on curiosity and connection turn into a guessing game? Why do so many fear commitment while also fearing loneliness?*

THE FRUSTRATION OF EFFORT

Dating or even just filtering, when did this become so hard? One day, there is a spark, the next, it is dust and air. People are shy and under pressure, too, but when did effort disappear? When did showing care become a red flag? When did vulnerability turn unattractive? Or maybe they never wanted me in the first place. *Ghosting became the new closure. Effort turned optional.* Most of the time, I know my worth. Still, it is hard not to doubt. Deep down, I know the right lid exists for my pot (how we say it in Germany), with the right we will see us, match our energy, meet me halfway. Side note: It is just frustrating that finding them feels like solving an emotional puzzle with no instructions.

WHERE DID THE MIDDLE GO?

Social media paints extremes. On one side, a perfect couple, equal, glowing in golden-hour light. On the other hand, endless posts declaring men are trash or that dating is broken. *Where did the middle ground go?*

In my eyes, partnership should be collaboration, not competition. Equality is not sameness, it is shared effort. Wanting to be treated like a queen also means treating the other person like a king. Relationships thrive on mutual investment, not imbalance. Still, in many scenes, dating rewards detachment. In a performative culture of filters and quick thrills, there is a surplus of beauty and a shortage of depth. Some offer little effort and still receive attention, others withhold emotion, mistaking distance for strength. That imbalance breeds surface-level intimacy, exciting outside, hollow underneath. Maybe that is why "*I do not chase, I attract*" resonates so deeply. It is not arrogance, it is exhaustion, self-respect in a world that confuses detachment with confidence.

Dating in your 20s today feels divided: hyper-romanticised on one side or how we call it "Love-Bombing", deeply cynical on the other. The quiet, honest middle where love grows slowly, without performance or fear, is rare. Most stories end not in closure but in limbo. It makes me wonder: *When did dating become an endless almost?*

If dating is defined by confusion, the antidote is transparent, direct, human communication. Signals get mixed, boundaries blur, emotions run deep. Honesty protects peace.

THOUGHTS RUNNING FREE

Being clear about feelings does not make you
"too much." It makes you emotionally literate.
Every awkward message is a small act of courage.

I once tried transparent communication with someone I was dating. Three dates. Three good days. Nothing dramatic, nothing rushed. We had not even kissed yet. Everything felt easy, aligned, calm, until suddenly it didn't. After our last date, something shifted. I could feel it before I could name it. Messages slowed. Energy changed. Then silence. Almost a full week of it. No explanation, no clarity, just a quiet disappearance into nothing. And that was the part that hurt the most, not the rejection, but the void. What later became clear was that one small thing about me did not match his vision. One detail. Not something that would have changed the future, not something unsolvable, just something imperfect. Instead of saying that, he chose distance. And I remember thinking how strange it is that so many things can align: values, interests, conversations, even visions and still one minor mismatch can outweigh everything else.

That moment taught me something important: clarity matters more than comfort. I would rather hear, "This doesn't feel right for me," than be left guessing, rereading messages, filling silence with self-doubt. So instead of disappearing too, I chose honesty. Not to convince him. Not to get an answer I could live with. Just to stay aligned with myself. I wrote something like this:

> "*Hey, sorry for getting back to you only now. I have been thinking about the last messages and was not sure whether to text at all. But since I want to improve my communication, it feels right to say this, mainly because we talked about transparency. After our last date, something felt different, and I am unsure what changed. I get that you had a whole week, truly, but what is missing for me is effort, or at least clarity. If you are no longer interested, that's fine, a heads-up would have been nice. :) For only three dates, I have thought about this far too much not to be honest.*"

Was it vulnerable? Yes. Did it feel uncomfortable? Absolutely. But it also felt clean. I did not betray myself by staying quiet just to appear "chill." I did not shrink to protect someone else's comfort. And here's the thing I remind myself of now: if someone is right for you, you cannot say the wrong thing. You cannot scare them off by being honest. You cannot lose them by asking for clarity. If that conversation ends the connection, then the connection was never stable to begin with. In a way, this situation became proof not of failure, but of alignment. Because if he had been the person for me, I wouldn't be writing about this here. I wouldn't be turning it into a lesson. It would have unfolded naturally, without silence, without guessing, without needing to translate absence.

If communication like this feels hard for you, you're not alone. Most of us were never taught how to express needs without apologising for them. That's why I created a few simple templates in this chapter, tools, not scripts. Ways to speak clearly without being harsh. To name needs without demanding. To choose honesty without self-abandonment. Because wanting clarity does not make you needy. Wanting effort does not make you dramatic. And asking for communication does not mean you're asking for too much. It just means you're asking the right person.

PAUSE & THINK

How does it feel to express emotion versus keeping it inside?

What changes when honesty becomes self-respect instead of exposure?

COMMUNICATION DRILL

Before reacting, disappearing, or overthinking, pause and practice intentional communication.

Clarity Without Apology

Write a message that does all three:

- Acknowledges delay or awkwardness
- States feelings clearly
- Asks for honesty or clarity without over-explaining

Template: "*Hey, I've been thinking about our last messages. It feels like something shifted. I understand busy weeks, but I am missing clear effort or communication. If you're not interested, that's okay, please just be upfront. I am looking for consistency and clarity.*"

This is not confrontation. It is alignment.

1. VULNERABILITY & INTENSE EMOTIONS

Vulnerability is often misunderstood as being dramatic. In reality, it is simply emotional honesty without performance.

Real Message Example: "*Hi, I've been trying to wrap my head around what happened on Friday. Seeing you unexpectedly threw me off. I wasn't upset because I saw you—I was upset because I didn't expect to still care that much. I am not angry. Just... human.*"

Naming the feeling removed its power to spiral.

EXERCISES

Emotional Mapping	**Transparency Practice**	**Digital Boundaries**
Notice where emotions show up first (chest, throat, stomach, shoulders).	Write one message that names a feeling without apology or justification.	Mute, unfollow, or pause rather than checking their story at 2 a.m.

THOUGHTS RUNNING FREE

Vulnerability is uncomfortable but transformative.
Naming what hurts turns emotion into awareness,
and awareness into growth.

EMOTIONAL COMMUNICATION

Answer honestly.

How comfortable am I expressing needs directly?

(Never) 0 — 1 — 2 — 3 (Often)

How often do I assume others should know how I feel?

(Never) 0 — 1 — 2 — 3 (Often)

How often do I rewrite or delay messages out of fear of being "too much"?

(Never) 0 — 1 — 2 — 3 (Often)

Higher scores do not mean weakness. They mean awareness.

---

2. FEAR BENEATH COMMUNICATION

Avoidance often hides fear, not indifference.

EXERCISES		
Fear Map	**Self-Dialogue**	**Reframe**
Trace one recurring fear to its origin.	Let your critical voice speak. Then let your compassionate voice respond.	Choose one past relationship. Write what it taught, not what it took.

THOUGHTS RUNNING FREE

Facing fear is not about erasing it. It is about understanding it deeply enough to move forward with grace rather than guarding yourself from life.

3. INTEGRATION — MODERN DATING AS A MIRROR

Dating, social media, and communication patterns mirror how you relate to uncertainty. Every instance of:

- overthinking
- withdrawal
- silence reveals something still asking for care.

REFLECTION METHOD

1. Label the emotion.
2. Name its source (present or past).
3. Define your direction.
4. Rewrite the moment with honesty and calm.

I HIT SEND. MY CHEST TIGHTENS. TOO MUCH?
OR MAYBE JUST ENOUGH TO FINALLY BE REAL.

AM I ATTRACTED OR JUST HORNY?

I WROTE THIS CHAPTER BECAUSE OF A FAMILIAR situation that kept repeating itself. There was someone at work, and a crush slowly formed. Nothing dramatic, nothing extraordinary. Just that quiet question that starts circling in your head: *Am I actually attracted to this person, or do I just feel horny?*

It made me realise how often desire sneaks in disguised as meaning, especially in environments where proximity, routine, and chemistry blur together. Work crushes, shared shifts, lingering looks, late conversations. They can feel intense without being deep. This chapter came from learning to pause in those moments and ask myself what I was really responding to: the person in front of me, or the sensation they awakened. Sometimes I cannot tell if I am into someone or just into the idea of being wanted. Attraction, loneliness, curiosity, and hormones blur together until it is hard to know what is real. Is this chemistry or just biology being dramatic again? Sometimes my body still acts as it did in its teens, thinking with hormones first, but the heaviness of the twenties is catching up, telling me to listen to my heart first.

THOUGHTS RUNNING FREE

Maybe I was not in love. Maybe I was just lonely.
Or curious. Or human. And perhaps that is okay
as long as I do not mistake chemistry for compatibility.

I have started calling it the 48-hour rule. When I meet someone and instantly feel that pull, I give it time. If I still want to talk to them after two nights of sleep, it is attraction. If not, it was probably just my body saying, "*Hey, I am alive.*" Desire loves to disguise itself as depth. A late-night text feels like destiny. A kiss feels like a connection. But sometimes it is just dopamine doing dress-up. Alcohol does not help. Under neon lights, everyone glows a little differently. But the morning always tells the truth, whether the connection was real or just really convenient. There is nothing shameful about desire. It is a pulse that reminds you are human. The trick is learning when it is curiosity and when it is a craving that passes as soon as it is met. Maybe maturing and healing means pausing before acting on impulse and asking: "*Do I want them or do I just want to feel something right now?*". Because wanting is not wrong but confusing it with connection is how people end up calling strangers soulmates after one drink. Desire starts stories, but communication decides how they end. Attraction might light the match, but honesty with us and others decides whether it burns or warms. Maybe that has the real lesson of modern dating: learning to tell the difference between what excites us and what sustains us.

PAUSE & THINK

Does attraction feel like a calm pull or a restless rush?

How often do you confuse attention with connection?

What usually happens after the rush fades, emptiness or peace?

How would desire feel if it were not tied to validation?

WHAT WE CALL CHEMISTRY IS SOMETIMES ATTACHMENT

People talk about chemistry like it is magic, as if that spark proves destiny. But I have started to wonder if what we call chemistry is sometimes just familiarity in disguise. A pull toward someone who feels exciting, intense, and alive, yet somehow ends the same way every time.

That flutter in your chest. The racing thoughts. The urgency you mistake for alignment. Sometimes it is not attraction at all. Sometimes it is anxiety dressed up as desire. Maybe your body is not recognising love, but remembering what chaos feels like. And because chaos once meant connection, you confuse tension for depth and intensity for intimacy.

THOUGHTS RUNNING FREE

It was not chemistry, it was recognition. Not of a soulmate, but of a pattern my body kept trying to heal.

I noticed that the people who made my stomach flip were often the same ones who kept my nervous system on edge. They felt intoxicating, but never steady. Familiar, but never safe. They felt like home only because they mirrored what my body learned to crave when certainty was missing. It took me a long time to realise that calm is not boring. That safety is not dull. That being understood quietly is a form of intimacy adrenaline cannot compete with.

I used to think love had to be electric to be real. Now I know real chemistry does not drain you. It steadies you. It does not leave you questioning your worth after every silence. It does not require decoding. It does not feel like a test you are constantly failing.

PAUSE & THINK

When does attraction feel grounding, and when does it feel destabilising?

Do you associate excitement with comfort or chaos?

Who feels like peace, and who feels like a pattern?

> THE SPARK IS NOT ALWAYS A SIGN. SOMETIMES IT IS JUST YOUR NERVOUS SYSTEM LIGHTING UP FOR WHAT FEELS FAMILIAR. HEALING IS LEARNING THAT CALM CAN FEEL LIKE A CONNECTION, TOO.

FROM CHEMISTRY TO CLARITY

ONCE YOU START SEEING PATTERNS FOR WHAT THEY are, something shifts. You stop chasing answers from the people who triggered them. You stop calling it unfinished business and start calling it awareness. Because sometimes what we crave is not the person, but the version of ourselves we became around them. The story we built. The meaning we assigned. The hope that this time it would end differently.

I used to replay conversations, analyse silences, and search for hidden meanings. I told myself I needed clarity, when what I really needed was honesty with myself. The truth was already there. I just kept negotiating with it. Awareness does not arrive dramatically. It arrives quietly, the moment you realise you are tired of repeating the same emotional lesson in different bodies.

This is the moment where attraction turns into information. Where longing turns into insight. Where you realise you are not broken for feeling deeply, you were just listening to the wrong signals.

CLOSURE IS NOT ALWAYS A CONVERSATION

We grow up believing closure means clarity. That one last conversation, explanation, or apology will calm the noise. That if they just explained themselves properly, we could finally move on. But sometimes closure does not sound like words. Sometimes it sounds like silence that finally stops hurting. I used to think closure lived in other people's honesty. If they could explain why it ended, why they changed, why they left, I would feel whole again. But closure is not something you receive. It is something you choose. Because what we really want from closure is validation. Proof that it mattered. Confirmation that we were not foolish for caring. And the truth is, you do not need anyone's permission for your feelings to be real.

THOUGHTS RUNNING FREE

I wanted closure. But what I needed was distance.
I wanted an ending. But what I found was acceptance.

Sometimes the apology never comes. The message stays unsent. The person who hurt you goes on living as if nothing happened. That is where closure becomes an act of self-respect. Choosing to stop explaining pain to someone who was never ready to understand it. Closure happens quietly. When you stop rereading messages. When you stop checking if they watched your story. When you stop writing imaginary replies to texts you will never send. One day, you realise the conversation already ended. You were just talking to the echo.

Maybe healing is not about tying everything up neatly. Maybe it is about learning to live with some unanswered questions without letting them control you. The story does not need to make sense to be complete.

PAUSE & THINK

What closure am I still waiting for and from whom?

What truth have I already accepted but keep resisting?

If I never got an answer, could I still choose peace?

CLOSURE IS NOT ALWAYS A CONVERSATION. SOMETIMES IT IS THE SILENCE THAT FINALLY LETS YOU BREATHE AGAIN. SOMETIMES IT IS THE QUIET DECISION TO STOP KNOCKING.

RELATIONSHIP CHECK-IN

YOU, ME, US

NONE OF THIS IS SCIENTIFIC. IT IS LIVED. THIS CHAPTER is not about labelling people as toxic or healthy. It is about noticing how relationships feel in your body and what they ask of you over time. Friendships, family ties, and romantic connections often mirror how regulated, valued, and honest you are with yourself. When something feels off externally, it is often because something internally is being ignored or overridden go.

FRIENDSHIP CHECK-IN

Toxicity is not limited to romance. It can look like emotional dumping, someone who always unloads but rarely checks how you are holding up. For a long time, I listened. I held space. I tried to be present through countless voice notes, long messages, and repeated cycles of the same pain. And then one day, I realised I did not have the capacity anymore not because I stopped caring, but because I had been carrying more than was mine.

A friend once texted, "I need to talk." I replied, "Sorry, I am at a birthday." She answered, "Ach so." In German, it loosely translates to "oh, I see", a small phrase that sounds neutral but often carries quiet disappointment or passive judgment depending on context. That single word used to trigger guilt. Now it signals imbalance.

You can care deeply and still reach your limit. You can listen for a long time and still decide to stop. Compassion does not require self-abandonment. Boundaries do not make you a bad friend, they make you an honest one.

FAMILY CHECK-IN

Family love can be unconditional, yet not always gentle. For me, it often appeared as a casual remark about my appearance in a photo online. I used to laugh it off while shrinking inside. Now I remind myself: if it is not kind, it does not need to be said. Setting boundaries with family can feel rebellious, but it is also an act of self-respect. Their opinions reflect their lens, not my worth.

THOUGHTS RUNNING FREE

I used to think love meant giving everything.
Now I know love that costs my peace is too expensive.

RELATIONSHIP CHECK-IN

Inconsistency is a quiet red flag, adoration one day, distance the next. Love should not feel like guessing whether you still matter. You can be busy. You can be tired. You can have your own life. Just do not make me question my place in it. Healthy partnerships balance independence and presence. I do not want to be someone's world, I want to be their cherry on top and offer the same in return.

RELATIONSHIP AUDIT

What am I offering?

What am I receiving?

Which boundary protects both peace and openness?

HEALTHY BOUNDARIES

Rate each statement

I can say "no" without guilt.

(Never) 0 — 1 — 2 — 3 (Often)

I can express discomfort directly.

(Never) 0 — 1 — 2 — 3 (Often)

I do not chase inconsistency.

(Never) 0 — 1 — 2 — 3 (Often)

I protect my peace, even if it disappoints someone.

(Never) 0 — 1 — 2 — 3 (Often)

I value mutual effort over one-sided giving.

(Never) 0 — 1 — 2 — 3 (Often)

TOTAL SCORE: ___________

HOW TO READ YOUR RESULTS

0–5 → EMPATH

This range often belongs to people who feel deeply and give easily. You sense emotions quickly, sometimes before others even name them. You are generous with your time, energy, and understanding, but you may struggle to protect your own limits. Saying no can feel like rejection, and prioritising yourself can trigger guilt. This does not mean you are weak, it means you are highly attuned to others. The growth here lies in learning that empathy does not require self-sacrifice.

6–10 → BALANCER

This range reflects growing awareness. You can recognise your needs and the needs of others, even if you do not always act on them perfectly. Sometimes you hold boundaries, other times you bend them. You are learning through experience what feels sustainable and what quietly drains you. Balance is not static, and being here means you are actively figuring out how to care without losing yourself.

11–15 → GROUNDED

This range suggests a strong sense of emotional self-respect. You value connection, but not at the cost of your peace. You can say no without over-explaining and notice red flags without rationalising them away. Boundaries feel less like walls and more like clarity. This does not mean you care less, it means you have learned that healthy relationships feel steady, mutual, and safe.

No result is better than another. Each one simply shows where you are learning to stand.

THE BOUNDARY SCRIPT

Friends: "*Hey, I care about you, but I do not have the mental space right now. Can we talk when I can be fully present?*"

Family: "*I know you mean well, but comments like that do not help me feel supported.*"

Relationships: "*I do not need constant attention, but I do need consistency.*"

Self: "*This is not mine to carry. I can care and still let go.*"

BOUNDARIES ARE NOT BARRIERS TO LOVE, THEY ARE IT CONTAINER. THE RIGHT PEOPLE ARE NOT OFFENDED BY YOUR LIMITS — THEY RECOGNISE THEMSELVES WITHIN THEM.

YELLOW

YELLOW

IT WAS MY FIRST DAY ALONE IN MONTHS. MY FRIEND Saskia had just left for her new job, and suddenly the silence felt louder than ever. I wandered down to the bay until I found a yellow bench beneath the trees, overlooking turquoise water that shimmered under the North Queensland sun. Everything around me looked alive. Birds moved through the mangroves, and sunlight danced on the water. Everyone assumes moments like this feel like sunshine. The world was bright, but I was not.

I had travelled thousands of kilometres from the small German town where I grew up to this coastline, and still, sitting there, I felt hollow. Not lost, just emptied out. The kind of emptiness that comes after too many changes, too many goodbyes, and too much holding it together. The bench felt like a checkpoint between who I had been and who I was becoming.

So, I sat down and cried. Not the dramatic kind of crying. The quiet, tired kind. The kind that comes when you have been strong for too long and finally allow yourself to stop. It was the first time in weeks, maybe months, that I let myself feel without fixing. Nothing was wrong on paper. I was simply overwhelmed by the weight of change and all the small endings that come with growing up. That yellow bench became more than a place to sit. It became a space of honesty. A place where sadness, gratitude, fear, and relief were allowed to exist at the same time. I was not broken. I was not failing. I was human.

Later that day, the very first person I ran into was Sofia from Chile. My first roommate. One of my yellow people. She did not ask questions. She did not try to fix anything. She just hugged me. It was the kind of hug you do not realise you need until you are already inside it. It did not solve the sadness, but it softened it enough for me to keep going.

Much later, long after that day, I told my friend Enda about the yellow bench. We were talking, as we often do, about the things that sit heavy and unnamed. I told him how I had sat there, staring at the ocean, crying, breathing, and waiting for the heaviness to soften. I told him how the bench had become a symbol for me, a place where emotion did not need justification.

We talked about how everyone needs their own yellow bench moments. Those rare pauses where emotions are allowed to exist without being labelled or solved. Moments where you do not ask yourself what this feeling means or how long it should last. You simply let it be. I reminded him, and myself, that feeling deeply is not a weakness. Strength is not the absence of emotion. Strength is allowing emotion to move through you without shutting down. People can only meet you as deeply as they have met themselves. That is why solitude matters. Those quiet yellow bench pauses are where we learn to meet ourselves first, before expecting anyone else to understand us.

THOUGHTS RUNNING FREE

I sat on a yellow bench by the ocean and cried. Not because I was weak, but because I was ready to stop pretending. Maybe that is what healing looks like, letting yourself feel, even when the view is beautiful.

Yellow may not just be a colour. Maybe it is a statement. It is the light that appears after a storm, not because the world has changed, but because you finally dare to look at it differently. It is a reminder that brightness can exist even on grey days. Warmth does not always mean happiness. Sometimes it means hope.

That day taught me that beginnings often hide inside endings. It taught me that loneliness can be a teacher. It taught me that sadness can sit next to sunlight without cancelling either out. As I cried in the middle of paradise, the ocean still moved gently behind me. A bird called from the trees. Somewhere in that stillness, a quiet truth settled in. Everything I needed was already inside me. I still think of that yellow bench often. It is my symbol of honesty. It is a place for release, reflection, and renewal. I hope everyone finds their own version of it someday, whether it is a place, a person, or a quiet moment where truth finally feels safe.

PAUSE & THINK

When was the last time you allowed yourself to feel something without fixing it?

Where is your yellow bench, the place where you can exist without expectation or distraction?

Who in your life reminds you that stillness can also be strength?

EVERYONE NEEDS A YELLOW BENCH MOMENT,
A PLACE WHERE HONESTY MEETS HEALING,
AND WHERE EVEN SADNESS FINDS ITS LIGHT.

V

GROWTH, STILLNESS & CONNECTION

Where restlessness turns into direction, and resilience learns softness. Every ending is also an evolution, not a finish line, but a deeper beginning.

THE HUMAN REALISATION

THERE IS A MOMENT IN YOUR TWENTIES WHEN YOU begin to understand something that sounds simple but changes everything: everyone, regardless of age or experience, is figuring it out in real time.

The people you admired as a child, the adults who once seemed unshakeable, and even those who appear confident today all carry insecurities and hidden battles. No one has an instruction manual. Most people are improvising, adjusting, learning, and hoping they are making the right decisions along the way. Everyone is doing their best with the tools they were given. It sounds simple, but it shifts everything.

For a long time, I saw my parents as people who could not break. They were steady, predictable, and capable, at least in my eyes. When they separated, that image cracked. Not dramatically, but clearly. I began to see them not as roles, but as individuals. Their separation showed me that adults experience heartbreak, confusion, and exhaustion just as deeply as anyone else. They are not superheroes. They are people navigating circumstances with the same uncertainty the rest of us carry.

Watching them struggle did not make them smaller. It made them real.

The more I paid attention to it, the clearer something else became to me: *every single person walking this earth is here for the first time*. Not just spiritually, depending on what you believe, but as the exact person they are right now. No one has lived this version of life before. No one has a blueprint. We all assume our problems are unique. We believe we are the only ones overthinking, doubting, spiralling, hoping, or *feeling behind*. But we never are

Many of the fears I carried in my twenties came from believing I was alone in them. The fear of not being enough. The pressure to make the "right" decisions. The constant self-questioning. Anxiety showed up in ordinary moments and felt intensely personal. Over time, I realised it was not unique at all. Almost every honest conversation revealed that others carried similar thoughts, even if they expressed them differently. The belief that "*no one else feels this way*" is one of the most isolating illusions of the twenties, and it is rarely true.

THOUGHTS RUNNING FREE

Everyone is trying. Everyone is learning.
Everyone is human, including me.

I want you to try something: *grab a piece of paper and a pen, do it old school if you can.* Or use whatever you like. *Write down one thing you always thought only you struggled with.* **A fear. A habit. A thought you are ashamed of. A feeling you have never said out loud.**

Now pause. *How many people do you think have felt the same way today alone?*

The problem does not disappear, but it becomes lighter. It pulls you back into reality. *Humans are allowed to struggle. Humans are allowed to break and rebuild. Humans are allowed to grow at uneven speeds. Your twenties make that visible.* You start noticing the cracks in everyone, even the people you once placed on pedestals. The person who intimidated you is insecure too. The friend who always gives advice sometimes cries in the shower. The coworker who looks confident online doubts themselves offline. Humanness levels us. It connects us more than anything else.

What surprised me most was how freeing that realisation became. I stopped expecting perfection from myself. I stopped assuming everyone else was doing better. And I stopped hiding so much. If everyone is figuring it out, there is no reason to pretend otherwise.

Being human is messy. Being human is beautiful. Being human is universal. And if there is one truth that anchors this chapter, it is this: **you are not alone**. Not in your fear. Not in your mistakes. Not in your confusion. Not in your becoming. We are all new here. We are all learning.

This chapter exists to remind you that you do not need to solve life perfectly to be doing it right. You are allowed to learn slowly. You are allowed to get it wrong first. You are allowed to have days when emotions make no sense or decisions feel heavier than they should. These experiences do not place you behind anyone else. They place you exactly where every other human stands, somewhere between knowing and learning. Being twenty-something is less about certainty and more about resilience. Less about having answers and more about asking better questions. Less about appearing composed and more about accepting the moments when you are not.

Everyone is doing their best with the tools they have, the experiences they carry, and the fears they rarely speak about. When you truly understand that, you stop expecting perfection from yourself and from others. You begin to see people, including yourself, not as symbols of what they should be, but as humans doing their best in real time.

BEING HUMAN IS NOT A FLAW. IT IS THE BASELINE. YOU ARE NOT BEHIND. YOU ARE NOT AN EXCEPTION. YOU ARE SIMPLY LEARNING, LIKE EVERYONE ELSE, ONE HONEST STEP AT A TIME.

PAUSE & THINK

What belief about yourself softens when you remember others feel the same?

Who did you place on a pedestal, and what changed when you saw their humanity?

What pressure could you release if you accepted that no one is doing life "correctly"?

A QUIET REALITY CHECK

Write down one thought you are convinced only you have. Not the polished one. The real one. The fear, habit, or belief you rarely say out loud. **Now pause.**

Imagine this exact sentence written by someone your age. A stranger. A friend. Someone you care about.

Would you judge them for it? Or would you understand?

If you would offer them compassion, patience, or reassurance, ask yourself why you deny yourself the same grace. That is the realisation. Not that the thought disappears, but that it was never yours alone.

RESILIENCE, RESTLESSNESS & REDEFINING SUCCESS

SUCCESS IS OFTEN MEASURED IN MILESTONES: degrees, promotions, relationships, numbers on a screen. But the older I get, the more I realise that resilience has less to do with achievement and more to do with recovery, with how gently we return to ourselves after falling apart. For a long time, I believed resilience meant staying strong, pushing through, performing, pretending everything was fine. But true resilience is quieter. It does not roar. It breathes. There were months when I could not tell whether I was exhausted or just empty. I told myself I only needed rest, but the truth was more profound: I had built my worth around motion. Around doing, fixing, and achieving. When I finally slowed down, I panicked. Stillness felt like failure.

Restlessness used to make me feel broken. I moved cities, changed jobs, booked flights, and searched for meaning in motion. But maybe restlessness is not failure. Maybe it is the body's way of signalling that growth is still happening, that the chapter is not over yet.

I started to realise that the reason I overthought everything was not weakness, but disconnection. When you forget what is yours, you begin measuring life by what belongs to everyone else. At some point, I hit a wall. I thought I was sad about someone else, but in truth, I was avoiding the person in the mirror. I kept chasing external validation, messages, attention, and being chosen, believing that recognition meant I was enough. But love that depends on constant reassurance is a fragile way to survive.

So, I stopped. *I stopped scrolling for proof that I mattered. I stopped rehearsing conversations in my head. I stopped outsourcing meaning*. And something shifted. The voice that once whispered, "*you are not enough*" began to fade, because I finally listened to another one, the quieter voice that said: You are okay. **You are learning. You are allowed to be.**

There is a part of resilience that is rarely talked about: the kind that does not come from within, but from the people who refuse to let you disappear.

For almost seven years, I was addicted to Snus, nicotine pouches that had quietly woven themselves into my daily life. I tried to quit more times than I can count. Every attempt failed. It was easy to excuse because it was common where I lived, especially in Sweden, but the people around me were never fans of it. Not because they judged me, but because they wanted better for me.

When I was living in Sweden, my friend group started having these spa days, slow, grounding rituals that felt almost ironic against how fast everything else moved. One day, while we were there, Serge and Stef looked at me and said, very calmly, very seriously: "Lea, you're stopping Snus today."

I laughed. I said no. They didn't. They took it away from me. Cold turkey. Completely. I had one pack hidden, with three left. I finished those and stopped, not on the Sunday I planned, but on the Monday that arrived anyway. It was intense. Uncomfortable. Messy. But what stayed with me was not the withdrawal. **It was the care that followed.**

THOUGHTS RUNNING FREE

For years, I thought I had to earn peace. Now I know it was waiting all along beneath the noise, in the quiet choice to let myself be supported.

Every day, my friends Serge, Stef, and Robin checked in with me. They reminded me *how strong I was. How proud they were.*

How much money I was saving. They told me to keep going when my body wanted to bargain.

Serge, especially, showed up in ways that had nothing to do with discipline and everything to do with care. He wrote me small quizzes, playful ones, where every answer was "**I am proud**." He texted me daily, not to monitor me, but to remind me I wasn't doing it alone.

Two years later, I am Snus-Free. I have no urge to start again. Not because I suddenly became stronger than everyone else, but because I was held long enough to become steady. That experience taught me something essential: resilience is not always self-made. Sometimes it is borrowed. Sometimes success looks like letting people care for you before you know how to care for yourself. Sometimes resilience looks nothing like strength. It looks like waking up, brushing your teeth, and showing up again. It is softer than motivation and quieter than ambition. Resilience is not loud, it is steady.

Over time, I have learned that excessive thinking subsides when you live in harmony with your values. When you stop deceiving yourself, there is nothing left to analyse, only the truth.

Now, when I make decisions, I trust them. Not because I am fearless, but because I am honest. When something feels right in my chest, I no longer need to justify it. Resilience is not about endurance. It is about gentleness showing up in your own life, even when the answers are unfinished. Maybe success is not about becoming unbreakable. It is about learning how to bend without losing yourself. And maybe restlessness is not something to fix; it is simply life nudging you forward. The other day, I was swimming with my friend Sara when we ran into Jane. While we stood talking, I found myself staring at the shells scattered along the shore. Their quiet symmetry pulled me back to a scenic flight over the Whitsundays, how everything looked from three thousand feet above.

From that height, Whitehaven Beach shimmered like glass. People moved like ants. All the things that usually take up so much space, body, hair, laughter, money, and health, disappeared. What stayed was perspective. We matter. Our choices ripple. Our presence counts. And yet, we are small inside something vast. Somehow, holding both truths at once makes life more meaningful, not because we are everything, but because we are part of everything.

This was not about strength. It was about learning how to return to myself, again and again.

Before you move on, notice what this chapter stirred. Resilience often reveals itself quietly.

PAUSE & THINK

When was the last time you rested without guilt?

Does resilience mean endurance, softness, or learning to accept help?

What feels heavy right now that might look smaller from a distance?

BORROWED STRENGTH

Write down the name of one person who stood beside you during a time when you could not stand alone.

ANSWER THESE QUIETLY:

What did they do that helped, even if it felt small?

Did you ever thank them in the way you wanted to?

What part of you became steadier because they stayed?

NOW REVERSE IT:

Whose steadiness have you been for someone else, without realising it?

Resilience is rarely a solo act. Notice where it was shared.

RESILIENCE IS NOT ALWAYS ABOUT PUSHING THROUGH. SOMETIMES IT IS ABOUT LETTING SOMEONE STAND NEXT TO YOU AND SAYING, "YOU DON'T HAVE TO DO THIS ALONE."

THE POWER OF CONNECTION

THIS CHAPTER IS ABOUT THE PEOPLE YOU MEET ALONG the way, brief or lasting, who change you, redirect you, and shape who you are becoming.

Every journey I have taken across countries, cities, and moments has shown me one truth: **connection gives life its shape**. It is the thread that weaves meaning through every chapter of becoming. Some of the most important bonds in my life began by accident: a stranger at a bus stop, a shared meal in a hostel kitchen, a conversation at an airport gate. You never really know when the next person you meet will change your life a little.

It started in 2018 with a ticket to Iceland, the first step into the unknown. That trip was meant to continue in Canada. I lasted four days before immigration closed that door. Instead of returning home, I said yes to another path, six weeks across the United States with people I had met once while working my mini job at Burger King. It sounds impulsive now, but it was one of the best decisions I ever made. From there, one moment led to the next, and each person I met shaped a small part of who I became.

After my six-week stay in America, I was waiting at San Francisco International Airport for my flight to Australia when I met Sharon. Two women at two very different turning points in their lives. She was newly divorced and flying to Taiwan to undergo treatment for MS. I was twenty, clutching my working holiday visa papers, scared but full of joie de vivre. We sat in front of the security checkpoint for five hours, two strangers with nothing to prove and nowhere else to go. We talked about pain, love, fear and new beginnings. This meeting taught me that connection is not bound by time, place or age, but by presence. Sometimes two lives intersect just long enough to leave an impression that lasts for years.

Curly, Cosma, Lisa, Macey, Ally, Frida and Valeria, my rays of sunshine. Each of them radiates a different kind of light: Curly, whose laughter transforms heaviness into lightness; Cosma, who listens with quiet grace; Macey, whose honesty feels like home; Ally, whose love never fades; Frida, whose curiosity keeps pushing me forward; Valeria, who wishes me success in every situation and reminds me to take my light with me wherever I go; and Lisa, who, even after years of separation, still brings warmth to my day with her voice. They are the kind of friends who clap the loudest when I am not in the room, even if they're on the other side of the world. That kind of loyalty doesn't fade with distance.

THOUGHTS RUNNING FREE

A stranger today. A soulmate tomorrow.
Maybe belonging is not a place. Maybe it is a person.

And then there are all the people I met along the way, the fleeting encounters in hostels, airports and late-night conversations that still echo in my memory. Every meeting, whether short or long, gave me something that reminds me that kindness is contagious, that souls can meet for a moment and still leave a light behind.

All the souls in Airlie Beach and on the Island taught me that connection is not always loud or visible. Sometimes it is the quiet check-in, the steady calm in the chaos, the safe space where truth does not have to be edited. They reminded me that honesty does not have to be heavy, that people who meet you in your vulnerability without fear are the ones to keep close.

And then there is the invisible web, the people who came and went, who were part of my village for a season. They helped me heal, held space when I did not know how to ask, or taught me something through conflict. It really does take a village to build a life. Not just to raise a child, as the saying goes, but to raise yourself.

Connections became both anchors and springboards. Anchors, because they reminded me that I was never truly alone. Springboards, because they pushed me into experiences I might never have found on my own. Every person I have met in airports, cafés, hostels, and workplaces has become part of that village. Some for a moment, some for years. But each left something behind: a word, a lesson, a kindness. I have realised that connection is the currency of resilience. It is what carries you when you feel untethered, what reminds you that even if you do not know where home is, you are still held by invisible threads of care. Friendship is easier to feel than to define. Let these questions remind you of who already shows up.

PAUSE & THINK

Who challenges you in a way that helps you grow, not shrink?

Which connection changed you in a way you did not expect?

How has connection carried you through homesickness, uncertainty, or change?

ADVICE FOR YOU

Try to think of one connection in your life that started in an unexpected place, a train ride, a random classmate, or someone you met while travelling.

Write down what that connection has given you: Perspective, support, growth, or laughter. Then ask yourself: *how can you nurture it further?*

When travelling or even just living, make it a practice to: Say yes to one invitation that feels slightly out of your comfort zone. Share one honest story about yourself with someone new. Keep a small connection journal where you note names, moments, and lessons from people you meet along the way.

The truth is that connection is the difference between feeling like you are drifting and realising you are being carried.

THE MOMENTS THAT MATTER MOST WERE NEVER PERFECTLY PLANNED. THEY WERE CONVERSATIONS THAT BEGAN WITH NOTHING BUT OPENNESS. A STRANGER'S KINDNESS. A SHARED STORY. A REMINDER THAT WE ARE NEVER REALLY ALONE IN THIS WORLD.

THE VILLAGE YOU BUILD

THIS CHAPTER IS ABOUT THE PEOPLE WHO STAY, THE ones who feel like home, and how belonging is built through care, effort, and time.

Something I cannot emphasise enough: **stick with people who feel like sunshine**. People who want to see you succeed. People who want to see you happy. People who love you.

Realising that everyone is human, including the people you once relied on the most, naturally leads to another truth: *none of us gets through life alone*. Whether we want to admit it or not, we are shaped by the people who walk with us, leave us, teach us, and love us in ways we do not always notice in the moment. We become a collection of influences, lessons, and echoes. A village, built slowly, unintentionally, and often without realising it.

Some people arrive quietly and end up shifting everything. Others stay for a season and teach you precisely what you needed to learn, even if their chapter in your life was short. *Some test your boundaries. Some show you what loyalty feels like. Some challenges you face in growing. Some make life less heavy*. And all of them, in several ways, leave fingerprints on who you become.

I think of Lisa, my best friend who has not been physically in my life for years, yet feels closer than most people I see daily or weekly. Her presence reminds me that connection does not require proximity, it requires intention. And then there are the fleeting interactions, the hostel roommates, the airport conversations, the people whose names I may have forgotten but whose influence I still feel. The strangers who became safe spaces. The friends who became family. The ones who did not stay but still mattered. Over the years, I have learned that you do not always choose your village. Sometimes it chooses you. The right people find you at the exact moment you need to grow into a new version of yourself. And the wrong people fall away when their lesson is complete.

Distance, timing, and different life seasons do not erase what was real. Not every friendship is meant to stay close forever, but many are meant to stay meaningful. Learning this helped me stop measuring connection by frequency and start recognising it by effort, care, and presence when it truly matters.

THOUGHTS RUNNING FREE

Maybe we do not grow alone at all. Perhaps we grow because someone, somewhere, believed in us when we could not yet see ourselves.

One of the strangest and most beautiful aspects of life in your beings of twenty-something is noticing how much of yourself comes from the people you know. Sometimes I catch myself saying something in a way an old friend always said it, using an expression from someone I haven't spoken to in years, or responding with a gentleness I learned from someone new. And in those moments, I realise: **I really am a mosaic of everyone I have ever loved**. Pieces of people I have met, trusted, admired, or healed alongside live quietly in me, in my voice, my habits, my humour, my resilience. That is the gift of connection: even when people leave, their influence does not disappear. *It becomes part of your architecture*. That is why the village you build matters so much.

It is not about the quantity of people in your life. It is about the quality of them. It is about those who check in without a reason. The ones who hold space for your confusion. The ones who challenge you with care, not criticism. The ones who want to see you win, even when they are not in the photo. These are the people who keep you human when life gets heavy. They are the reminders, the grounding forces, the quiet anchors.

And sometimes, you will be that person for someone else, the calm voice, the honest friend, the safe place to land. That is the beauty of real connection: **when it is genuine, it is never one-sided.**

When I think about growth now, I do not picture milestones or achievements. I picture people. The ones who helped me see myself more clearly. The ones who reflected parts of me I had forgotten. The ones who stayed steady when everything else felt uncertain. My village is not perfect, but it is real. And that is enough.

A village is not made up of those who are constantly around you, but those who are still a part of you, even when life pulls you apart.

PAUSE & THINK

Who in your life feels like sunshine?

How can you nurture your village with the same care you hope to receive?

What kind of village are you building around yourself?

YOUR VILLAGE, RIGHT NOW

Take a moment and list five names. Not the people you see most often. The people who feel safe.

Next to each name, write one word:

- **what they bring into your life**
- **or what part of you they helped shape**

Now look at the list. Notice who stayed. Notice who changed. Notice who may no longer be present, but still lives in you. This is your village in its current form. It is allowed to evolve.

YOU ARE ALLOWED TO BUILD A VILLAGE THAT FEELS LIKE HOME AND TO OUTGROW THE ONES THAT DO NOT.

VI
SHIFTS AND SHADOWS

Where the world slowed down and the inner world spoke louder than ever.

THE PAUSE
COVID-19 YEARS

COVID-19 BROUGHT THE WORLD TO A STANDSTILL and intensified inner realities. It altered friendships, routines and perceptions of time. The silence was both frustrating and transformative, a collective pause that forced us to reflect, taught us patience and showed us how fragile, yet adaptable, everyday life really is.

I remember just returning home from a year abroad filled with travel, discovery, and the rush of independence. I had started my degree, moved to a new city, and was only beginning to understand what it meant to live on my own. Life finally felt like movement: *studying, exploring, building something new*. Then, half a year later, came the news of a virus spreading somewhere in Asia. We thought it would stay distant. We still had one semester, one carnival, one more carefree moment before everything stopped.

And then *pause*.

The world shut down. Streets went silent, cities slowed, and time seemed to stretch and collapse all at once. What was supposed to be a few weeks became months, then years. Between early 2020 and 2022, everything blurred. Age froze somewhere between the early and mid-twenties, as if growing older no longer followed the passage of time but rather the unfolding of circumstances.

Those years became a strange mix of survival and stagnation. I worked, studied, and tried to create a routine that felt like progress, even when nothing moved. I moved in with my ex, got two cats, the so-called COVID-19 pets that everyone either got instead of babies or alongside them. I chose wisely.

But when I look back, it is as if I blinked, and suddenly it was 2025. Somewhere between the quiet mornings, online classes, cancelled plans, and long walks just to feel air, time dissolved. The twenties, those supposed years of energy, movement, and connection, turned into a silent classroom of patience and inner reflection.

I think many people felt that same strange dislocation, the sense of having aged but not lived, of having changed but not moved. COVID-19 did not just stop the world, it changed how time felt. It slowed growth but also deepened awareness. It taught how to sit with uncertainty, how to be with oneself, and how easily everything taken for granted can disappear.

THOUGHTS RUNNING FREE

Sometimes I forget I am twenty-something. COVID-19 made four years feel like nothing. Did I miss my youth, or am I still in it?

When the world finally reopened, it was not about "returning to normal." It was about learning to live again, but with a quieter understanding of what truly matters. The pandemic created a collective pause and a personal mirror. It stripped away distractions and forced confrontation with stillness, the kind of silence that reveals what has been ignored. Stillness can feel like loss, yet it often becomes the beginning of clarity.

PAUSE & THINK

What did stillness show about your priorities?

Who or what did you miss most when everything stopped?

Which parts of your life did not return when the world reopened, and why?

HOW HAS MY SENSE OF AGE CHANGED?

This exercise helps you notice how the pandemic reshaped your sense of age, time, and growth. It shows that development does not only happen through milestones, but also through pause, reflection, and emotional change. The goal is not to measure progress, but to understand how stillness shaped who you are becoming.

Instructions: Rate each statement on the scale provided. Use the space below each prompt to jot down a specific memory or thought that comes to mind.

0 = Not at all | 1 = Rarely | 2 = Somewhat | 3 = Strongly True

1. I feel older than my age because of what I experienced during the pandemic.

(Not at all) 0 — 1 — 2 — 3 (Strongly True)

A moment that made me feel "aged":

2. I sometimes forget how much time has passed since 2020.

(Not at all) 0 — 1 — 2 — 3 (Strongly True)

The hardest year for me to account for was:

3. I feel like my emotional age changed faster than my physical one.

(Not at all) 0 — 1 — 2 — 3 (Strongly True)

In what way do I feel "wiser" or "heavier"?

4. The pandemic years reshaped my priorities about work, love, and time.

(Not at all) 0 — 1 — 2 — 3 (Strongly True)

What used to matter that no longer does?

5. I find it harder to measure growth in milestones; I think in moments now.

(Not at all) 0 — 1 — 2 — 3 (Strongly True)

A small "moment" of growth I noticed lately:

6. I often feel younger again when reconnecting with things I missed during lockdown.

(Not at all) 0 — 1 — 2 — 3 (Strongly True)

The last time I felt like my "pre-2020 self" was:

7. I learned to value slower growth over quick success.

(Not at all) 0 — 1 — 2 — 3 (Strongly True)

One area where I am finally taking my time:

THE SYNTHESIS

Look back over your ratings. If you have many 2s and 3s, your "internal clock" has likely undergone a significant shift.

Write one word to describe your current relationship with time:

> THE WORLD PAUSED. BUT MAYBE,
> FOR A MOMENT, WE FINALLY LISTENED.

GROWING OLDER, STILL THE SAME

GROWING OLDER OFTEN COMES WITH AN UNSPOKEN assumption: *that time should turn us into someone else.* Wiser, calmer, more put together. Yet the longer I sit with the idea of age, the more I question whether we truly change at our core, or whether we simply learn how to carry ourselves differently. Perhaps growth is not about becoming a new person, but about slowly uncovering the one who was there all along. I do need to say that, I am curious how much of our personality profoundly changes over time. *Do we ever really become someone else, or do we grow into who we have always been?* Sometimes we look at children and think, like we already know who they will become.

And yet, twenty years later, the outcome surprises everyone. We often judge people by fragments of who they once were, the teenager still finding direction, the child still exploring. I believe our core personality rarely changes. Growth refines us, but it rarely replaces our essence. We age, learn, and soften, yet that inner spark, the self that existed before experience shaped us, remains. We grow older, but fundamentally, we remain ourselves. We have just become wiser versions.

THOUGHTS RUNNING FREE

One moment, I feel eighteen, laughing on the floor with friends. Next, I feel forty, worrying about rent. Maybe age is a mood.

Some days, we slip back two steps behind a lesson we thought we had learned. Other days, we stride forward, proud of the distance covered. Looking back, so much has already been achieved. So much has been lived. And yet, the same inner self still whispers underneath it all.

"I have always been her just steadier now, more aware, and prouder."

Maturity does not come automatically with age, but is acquired through experience, decisions and trials. Maturity does not come with birthdays or job titles, but unfolds in moments that test grace, boundaries and honesty. Being mature does not mean being perfect. For me, it means rising above what makes you feel small, even when comfort tempts you to stay.

It means being the "bigger person," not to gain recognition, but to find peace. It means knowing that people will talk, that promotions may pass you by, and still choosing integrity. Sometimes maturity is simply that: returning to your younger self and saying, "*You did your best. I am proud of you.*"

PAUSE & THINK

Maturity has little to do with numbers and everything to do with experience. Growing older is not about changing who you are but about deepening your understanding of the person you have always been.

WHAT MAKES YOU FEEL YOUNG? WHAT MAKES YOU FEEL OLD?

WHEN I FEEL YOUNG

- Laughing until my stomach hurts with friends.
- Letting my inner child feel safe and free.
- Going a day without overthinking.
- Jumping into rivers or puddles without caring who is watching.

WHEN I FEEL OLD

- The sudden arrival of lower-back pain.
- Thinking about investments and spreadsheets.
- Handling uncomfortable situations with calm instead of impulse.

Take five minutes and list your own.

MAYBE GROWING OLDER IS NOT ABOUT BECOMING SOMEONE NEW. IT IS ABOUT REMEMBERING WHO YOU HAVE ALWAYS BEEN AND MEETING THAT PERSON WITH MORE KINDNESS.

TEENAGE LESSONS, ADULT LIFE

GROWTH OFTEN COMES QUIETLY, DISGUISED AS change. Not the dramatic, cinematic kind, but the kind that makes you pause and realise that something inside you has changed, even if nothing looks dramatically different on the outside.

I was talking to my colleague Vici at work the other day, and she said something that stuck with me: living on the island made her feel like a **teenager again**. That thought stayed with me for days. It made sense. Every time we step into unfamiliar territory, we meet ourselves all over again. The uncertainty returns. The curiosity returns. The world feels bigger and less predictable, and suddenly we are students of life once more. Feeling like a teenager is not regression, but renewal. Every unfamiliar situation, a new job, a move, a change of heart, silently demands growth. We are forced to redefine our desires, test our limits and clarify what is really important. Somewhere in this process, we begin to recognise what we need, even if we don't yet know where we going.

This idea of growth led me to another realisation: some of the most meaningful developments arise not from movement but from distance. Recently, I spoke with one of my closest friends, Cosma, about what it is like to maintain a long-distance friendship. It is bittersweet. You live your life while the other person lives theirs, and when you meet again, you try to weave two separate stories back together. She asked the questions people ask when there is uncertainty in the air: "*When are you coming back? Are you going to stay? What are your plans?*" And my honest answer surprised even me. I said, "*I don't know.*"

THOUGHTS RUNNING FREE

I think feeling like a teenager again is not regression, it could be proof that life still excites me. Distance may not be a loss, but it may be a reminder that connection can stretch without snapping. Maybe growth is not about leaving or staying but about trusting that both can coexist.

Not knowing is uncomfortable, especially when your decisions affect people you love. It's hard to think selfishly when self-determination carries the risk of hurting someone else. When I talked to my other best friend, Curly, about it, she said gently, "If you want to stay, stay. I'll still be here, and you'll still be there." She reminded me that even if we both lived in Germany, we wouldn't see each other every day, just in different cities. That made me question something I had always taken for granted: *does living in the same time zone really make it easier to stay connected? Or is effort more important than geographical distance?*

Cosma saw it from a different perspective. She said "*we would probably see each other more often*" when I came back and even asked "*if our friendship could last that way.*" But behind all her questions, I could hear what she really wanted to say. **She misses me. And I miss her too.**

So I told her what I am slowly learning to accept about myself and life. We all live our own lives, and that doesn't mean we love each other any less. We can care deeply for each other without sharing the same place or pace. Sometimes growth requires us to expand across oceans, time zones, and growing versions of ourselves. Giving each other space doesn't always look like closeness. Sometimes it looks like trust.

PAUSE & THINK

When did you last feel like a beginner again?

What unfamiliar environment has recently tested or redefined you?

Who do you still carry with you even from afar?

Which friendships have stretched rather than broken with distance?

SO MANY EXCITING THINGS ARE HAPPENING. I DON'T WANT TO RUSH THEM. I WANT TO FOLLOW WHAT IS MEANT FOR ME WITH CARE, BUT WITHOUT STRESS. BECAUSE GROWTH DOESN'T ALWAYS SHOUT, SOMETIMES IT WHISPERS: YOU ARE STILL IN THE PROCESS OF BECOMING. KEEP GOING.

VII
THE REAL WORLD

Money, work, education,
and finding your footing.

HOME AND AWAY
MONEY, WORK & SURVIVAL

YOU CAN BE FREE AND BROKE, OR STABLE AND stuck, and both can be equally confusing. Adulthood does not come with a manual, it comes with invoices.

At first, earning your own money feels like freedom. It is proof that you are capable, responsible, and finally adult. One day, you celebrate your first pay check. The next, you calculate how much of it disappears into rent, taxes, or the extra oat milk you did not need but somehow always buy. Slowly, that sense of freedom shifts. Independence stops feeling romantic and starts feeling practical. What once symbolised possibility begins to resemble survival.

This is one of the quiet contradictions of being twenty-something. You are encouraged to **explore**, **travel**, **move**, **and dream**, yet you are also **expected to stay stable**, **save money**, and **build a future** at the same time. You cannot fully do both, but you try anyway. That tension sits beneath almost every financial decision.

Money, I learned, was never just about numbers. It was about safety, dignity, and the illusion of control. In my early twenties, I thought financial independence meant "*I do not need anyone*". Over time, I realised it often means learning how to ask for help differently. Not as failure, but as maturity.

Working across countries made that lesson unavoidable. In Germany, success was measured through job titles and structure. In Sweden, it showed up as balance and space to live. In Australia, success often meant how far a pay check could stretch before the next rent was due. There were nights I counted tips twice to make sure they would cover the week ahead. There were mornings I woke up proud that I was still figuring it out, one shift, one step, one sunrise at a time.

Being broke abroad humbles you. It teaches resourcefulness and gratitude, but it also introduces a kind of exhaustion that feels heavier than your age suggests. That exhaustion rarely shows up on a resume, yet it shapes you deeply. It teaches you what survival actually costs.

At the same time, there is a strange pride attached to being *busy*. As if exhaustion equals importance. I have worked sixty-hour weeks that looked impressive on paper and felt hollow in reality. I have also lived through months of stillness, when time stretched and life slowed, and those months taught me far more. Society glorifies the hustle but rarely the pause.

THOUGHTS RUNNING FREE

I am old enough to work full-time, but still young enough to panic when my card declines. Maybe growing up is just learning how to pretend you are not scared of the numbers, and maybe pretending is how we survive until we finally believe we can.

It took me years to understand that rest is not laziness, it is clarity. Some of my most productive moments happened when I stopped chasing and started listening. I think often of the Island. The long shifts. The steady rhythm of tourists arriving and leaving. The ocean always visible, yet just out of reach while standing behind the bar. Even there, between exhaustion and laughter, meaning appeared. Sometimes purpose is not found in passion projects. Sometimes it is found in doing what needs to be done to keep moving forward.

No one prepares you for the emotional math of adulthood. You gain independence but lose proximity. You gain confidence but lose simplicity. I remember sitting on the floor of my Airlie Beach apartment, surrounded by unpacked bags, visa papers, and overdue emails. The air-conditioning was broken. My bank account was nearly empty. I felt free and trapped at the same time. With that freedom comes guilt. The guilt of leaving. The guilt of staying. The guilt of knowing you cannot do both. We are told to chase opportunity, but we rarely talk about how heavy it feels to leave pieces of yourself behind. Sometimes the price of freedom is not money. It is loneliness.

For years, I believed success followed a straight line: graduate, get a job, get promoted, buy a house. Life has shown me something else. Growth is not linear. It is a spiral. You return to familiar places, but with different eyes.

Now, success looks quieter to me. *It looks like paying rent and still feeling alive. It looks like knowing when to rest without guilt. It looks like doing work that does not cost your soul.*

My background in sustainability keeps reminding me that sustainability is not only environmental. It is personal. A sustainable life is one you can emotionally afford. You cannot pour from an empty self, no matter how full your bank account appears. Maybe survival in your twenties is not about climbing faster. Maybe it is about learning how to breathe while you climb.

PAUSE & THINK

What does “financial independence” mean to me: freedom, control, or fear?

When was the last time I made a choice purely for security, not joy?

Do I measure success by income, or by how I feel when I wake up on a Monday?

SURVIVAL BUDGET VS. SOUL BUDGET

Take ten minutes to reflect on two sides of your life:

SURVIVAL BUDGET	**SOUL BUDGET**
Where your money goes.	Where your energy goes.

COMPARE THEM.

Are you investing in things that refill you, or just in things that keep you running?

If one small expense does not bring peace, maybe it costs more than it is worth.

FREEDOM FEELS LIKE THE OCEAN, VAST AND UNSTEADY. LEARNING TO FLOAT TURNS SURVIVAL INTO STRENGTH.

PARENTS, EXPECTATIONS & FINDING YOUR OWN PATH

She pushed me out the door.
I thought I was leaving home.
Turns out I was finding it.

WHEN MY MOTHER ENCOURAGED ME TO GO ABROAD as part of an exchange programme, I didn't understand what she really meant. She didn't just mean studying or travelling. She meant this: *go out into the world and find yourself without me being around.* At the time, I saw distance as a loss. Independence seemed like rebellion to me. Looking back, letting go can be a profound form of care and love. I remember travelling to the Dubai Expo with my mother during my bachelor's degree. This trip was special because education and life took place in the same place. Surrounded by innovations in sustainability, I noticed how her quiet curiosity mirrored my own. I was striving for independence, and she was watching me grow into it. That moment reminded me that parenting doesn't stop when a child becomes an adult. Parenting transforms into trust.

For a long time, I imagined my parents to be unbreakable. When they separated, that image shattered. The separation did not diminish them. The separation made them real. I began to see individuals behind the roles, with stories, boundaries, hurts and hopes. This change altered something in me. It changed my understanding of expectations.

Gratitude and boundaries can coexist. Love and disagreements can coexist. Adulthood begins when guidance feels like pressure. **Most families repeat the same argument in different costumes,** which means this pressure is personal, but it is not unique. For me, that pressure manifested itself the moment I made decisions that aligned not with the plans of others, but only with my own: where I wanted to live, what I wanted to study, who I wanted to love, and when I wanted to rest. Leaving home wasn't the hardest part. The hardest part was redefining what "*home*" meant to me after I moved out.

The true inheritance is not money. The true inheritance is behavioural patterns. The tone of voice during arguments. The silence after a disappointment. The way love is shown or withheld. The expectations that hang unspoken in the air. Every family teaches in its own language. Some teach resilience through struggle. Some teach care through overprotection. Some teach independence by letting go too soon. Understand that inheritance is not about guilt. Understand that inheritance is about choices. Choices determine what remains and what is overcome.

THOUGHTS RUNNING FREE

I used to think growing up meant proving them wrong.
Now it means understanding them and choosing differently,
without resentment.

My mother once said, "*I just want you to be happy.*" There was love in that sentence. And fear, too. Her definition of happiness included stability, routine, security. Mine included movement, curiosity, possibilities. Neither is wrong. Both belong to different generations living different realities.

We all carry invisible expectations with us. Finish your studies. Decide on a career. Build a life that looks good on paper. It's natural to want to make your parents proud. Sometimes, however, that means disappointing them in their plans for you.

Love can look like hidden fear: fear of losing you, fear that you will suffer, fear that you will choose a life they don't know.

I used to feel guilty for leaving and living a life that didn't match theirs. Today, I see a different decision less as a departure and more as an appreciation of the freedom that made my decisions possible. One generation creates stability so that the next generation can create opportunities. They built the house. I am learning to leave it without losing the love in it. The older I get, the more I see my parents as people, not as roles, not as expectations. As people. Maybe adulthood doesn't mean proving something. Maybe adulthood means understanding.

PAUSE & THINK

What expectations still feel heavy because they are not truly mine?

Where does love show up as care in my family, and where does it show up as fear?

Which pattern do I want to keep, and which pattern do I want to end?

> SHE PUSHED ME OUT THE DOOR.
> I THOUGHT I WAS LEAVING HOME.
> TURNS OUT I WAS FINDING IT.

THE EXPECTATION FILTER

Take a quiet moment and write down three expectations that still feel heavy. They might sound like:

"*I should stay close.*"
"*I should be more stable by now.*"
"*I should want what they want for me.*"

Next to each one, answer two questions:

1. Where did this expectation come from?
   (A parent, family culture, fear, tradition, love, habit.)
2. Does this expectation help me grow, or does it keep me small?

Now rewrite one of those expectations as a choice.

For example: "*I should stay close*" becomes "*I choose connection without sacrificing my direction.*"

You do not need to explain this choice to anyone yet. Clarity comes before communication.

DEGREE DONE — NOW WHAT?

CAP TOSSED. DEGREE IN HAND. INSTEAD OF CLARITY, there were only more questions.

The completion of my master's degree felt less like a celebration and more like an echo. I remember coming out of the final seminar and thinking that years of studying, stress, deadlines and ambition had collapsed into a single piece of work and a single moment that was supposed to feel like an arrival but didn't. There was no cinematic ending, no bombastic music, no inner peace. There was silence, exhaustion and an inbox full of rejection letters.

Education had shaped my life for years. It gave me structure, rewarded my efforts with grades, and clearly defined success. Then suddenly it was over. No more curriculum. No next assignments. No obvious next steps. Something that is supposed to prepare us for life often delays life itself. When people ask, "*What are you doing right now?*", the question sounds harmless, but it carries weight. It presupposes a direction, certainty and answers that are rarely available at this stage.

After completing my two degrees, I expected to feel pride. For a moment, I did. But underneath that was pressure. Everyone else seemed to be moving forward quickly, starting careers, earning titles and making polished announcements that sounded like victories. Progress seemed loud and public.

Meanwhile, I sat in Sweden with a half-packed suitcase, wondering what 'ready for work' actually meant. My education had given me knowledge, but no clarity. It taught me systems, theories and models, but not how to want something. That's the part that's rarely acknowledged: graduating from university is neither a failure nor a success. It's a space. An uncertain space between what you were and what you will become.

We are taught to treat graduation as a finish line. In reality, it is a door that is not easy to open. A degree does not automatically mean opportunities, identity or peace. Real learning begins when assessment disappears, when no one but yourself evaluates your progress. After the final exam, the noise fades away and a new silence emerges. This silence feels unsettling, but this is where self-determination begins to develop.

THOUGHTS RUNNING FREE

I thought finishing my degree would make me feel complete. Instead, it made me realise how unfinished I am, and maybe that is the point. Education gave me answers. Life gave me better questions.

I used to measure my life in semesters. Today, I measure it by the risks I have taken, the people I have met, and the moments that required courage. Education imparts information. Learning brings about change. At university, I studied sustainability, systems and development, but I learned the most formative lessons elsewhere:

- Negotiating a lease in another language
- Balancing work alongside full-time study
- Moving abroad without certainty
- Recognising burnout and choosing to pause

These experiences have shaped my resilience more than any textbook ever could. Much of our real education takes place outside of institutions, at airports, at work, through heartbreak and unexpected twists and turns. These lessons are not rewarded with certificates, but they stay with us longer.

PAUSE & THINK

What expectations did others have for you after graduation?

How many of those did you genuinely want for yourself?

What has education taught you beyond academics about discipline, identity, or limits?

THE POST-GRADUATION INVENTORY

Take a blank page and divide it into two columns:

WHAT I LEARNED		WHAT I ACTUALLY USE
Academic theories	→	Confidence to speak in public
Research structure	→	Adaptability under pressure
Time management	→	Knowing when to rest
Global perspectives	→	Gratitude for where I am

Now, underline the lessons that came outside the classroom. Those are your real degrees.

A REFRAME, NOT ADVICE

Stop rushing to define success.

You cannot measure it in months.

Life after graduation is not a race, it is a reset.

Let direction reveal itself.

Not all decisions are visible immediately.

Some paths appear only once you start walking.

Redefine productivity.

Rest, travel, or uncertainty are not wasted time,
they are invisible forms of growth.

Stay curious.

The most employable skill is adaptability.

The most human one is self-awareness.

EDUCATION ENDS WITH EVALUATION.
LEARNING CONTINUES WITHOUT PERMISSION.
NOT KNOWING IS NOT A GAP TO FILL. IT IS
A SPACE WHERE DIRECTION SLOWLY FORMS.

THE JOB JUNGLE

AFTER FINISHING MY DEGREE, I THOUGHT THE MOST challenging part was over. It was not. The real challenge began when I opened my laptop, ready to apply for jobs, and realised that no one was waiting. No one cared about my GPA, my thesis, or my idealism. The job portals felt endless, hundreds of listings that all demanded "three years of experience" for an entry-level role. I remember refreshing my inbox daily. Nothing. Then, one day, the dreaded line: "*We regret to inform you that we've decided to move forward with other candidates.*"

At some point, I stopped counting how many times I read that sentence. Job searching became its own kind of unpaid full-time job filled with hope, rejection, and endless self-questioning. I began to realise that education prepares you to think, but not to cope. No one teaches what it feels like to be qualified on paper but invisible in practice. And I realised that there is a strange emotional cycle that comes with early job hunting:

Excitement: *Maybe this one.*
Doubt: *I am not good enough.*
Rejection: *They did not even read my application.*
Exhaustion: *What is the point?*
Hope: *Okay, let us try again.*

It is humbling to realise how quickly confidence fades when success depends on someone else's "yes."

At first, I thought something was wrong with me. Then I realised: **it is not personal, it is systemic**. The job world today is built like a maze full of contradictions, keywords, and expectations that rarely match human reality. People often say, "**Welcome to the real world.**" But what they forget is that this world is also chaotic, exhausting, and full of contradictions. When I graduated, I thought I would enter sustainability or policy roles, something creative that blended purpose and impact. Instead, somehow, I landed in hospitality, administration, and side jobs that paid rent but not identity.

THOUGHTS RUNNING FREE

Another email: "We regret to inform you..."

But somehow, I still hope the next one says yes.

That could be what resilience really is: not pretending it does not hurt but showing up anyway. Education ended with a degree. But the real lessons began when life stopped grading and started testing.

And yet those "**in-between**" jobs shaped me more than any perfect title could have. They taught presence, discipline, empathy, and humility. They made me face people, not theories. At one point, I worked double shifts, half-dreaming about circular-economy strategies while serving cocktails and smiling through exhaustion. That is the paradox of your twenties: **building a resume and a life at the same time.**

Studying sustainability felt like a mission, working after it felt like negotiation. Suddenly, "**making a difference**" had to fit inside job descriptions, budgets, and corporate structures. I kept asking myself: "*Where is the line between survival and purpose?*"

Because it is hard to save the planet when rent is due on Thursday.

Nevertheless, I refused to let this disappointment destroy my ambitions. Instead, I began to understand sustainability differently, not just as a profession, but as a way of life. The balance between energy, resources and self-esteem became a form of circular economy in its own right. Living abroad adds another layer to the whole picture. Applying for a job as a foreigner involves invisible barriers, sponsorship, visa restrictions and small print that can reduce your chances in advance. Each rejection hit differently, not because of skill, but because of circumstance. I was not just competing for jobs, I was competing for permission to stay. But that experience built resilience. It taught me to fight for my space not through shouting, but through persistence, self-awareness, and faith that something meaningful would eventually match my effort.

PAUSE & THINK

What did you expect adulthood to look like, and how does it actually feel?

What does "career success" mean to you when no one is watching?

What can be learned from rejection that praise never teaches?

THE REFRAME TABLE

Circle the lesson that feels most relevant right now.
That is where your growth is happening.

Challenge	**What It Taught Me**	**Hidden Strength**
Job rejection	Patience	Self-worth not tied to approval
Working outside my field	Adaptability	Real-world skills
Visa uncertainty	Resilience	Long-term vision
Burnout	Boundaries	Balance between effort and rest

ADVICE FOR THE TRANSITION

Stop comparing your timeline. Everyone's pace is different. Some climb fast, others build deep, both. Both matters.

Let imperfection teach you. Every side job, delay, and detour adds texture. You are not behind, you are accumulating stories that will later become your experience.

Stay curious, not desperate. Desperation closes doors that curiosity opens. Ask, learn, volunteer, network, not for validation, but expansion.

Redefine purpose as progress. Maybe right now, purpose is paying rent, showing up, and not losing yourself. That counts too.

PERSONAL GROWTH & DISCIPLINE

DISCIPLINE IS NOT PUNISHMENT, IT IS A FORM OF SELF-respect. In your twenties, structure often feels like restriction, but in reality, it creates space for freedom. There is this unspoken myth that growth has to be dramatic: new jobs, new cities, new versions of yourself. But most of the time, real growth looks ordinary. It looks like showing up when no one is watching, keeping a promise to yourself, or saying no when something does not align.

The truth is simple: chaos does not build character. Consistency does. Most of the time, growth happens in quiet places: a morning walk, journaling instead of spiralling, stretching before bed, choosing a proper meal instead of another rushed snack. These small actions become acts of self-trust. Discipline is not about control, it is about commitment. It is not about perfection, it is about patience. Your twenties teach you that motivation comes and goes, but discipline stays. It is the bridge between intention and transformation.

For me personally, discipline became easier the moment my vision became clearer. I do not mean knowing every step or having a rigid five-year plan. I mean understanding the kind of life I want to live, the person I see myself becoming, the energy I want around me, and the future I am building toward. When that direction is clear, discipline stops feeling like pressure and starts feeling like alignment.

Even with that clarity, I still struggle with routines. Simple tasks overwhelm me sometimes. My newest routine is waking up and using a frozen cucumber on my face every morning, and honestly, it feels like an achievement. Not because it is a "wellness habit," but because it is something I do for myself. It makes me feel good. It makes me feel cared for by me. That has been the most significant shift: choosing habits that nourish me, not those that impress anyone else. For a long time, I felt pressure to follow the "right routines," the ones everyone online seems to have mastered. But I realised that when a habit is not right for me, it is not discipline. It is performance. Discipline only works when it is personal, when it grows from your values rather than expectations.

THOUGHTS RUNNING FREE

Some days discipline looks like ambition. Other days it looks like getting out of bed and choosing myself anyway. I am learning that consistency does not need to be loud to be real. It only needs to be mine.

So, I am learning to build habits that support my life, rather than trying to fit myself into habits that look good on the outside. I still procrastinate. I still get overwhelmed. I still forget routines. But I am not trying to be perfect, I am trying to be committed. The routine can be small. It can change. It can start with something as tiny as a cold cucumber in the morning. What matters is that I do it for me.

When your habits come from self-respect instead of self-pressure, discipline becomes less about controlling your life and more about creating a life that feels true.

Nobody posts the early alarms, the failed workouts, or the nights you choose rest instead of proving something. But those moments are often the turning points. Growth rarely looks impressive up closely, it only looks impressive in hindsight. When life feels unstable, the healthiest thing you can do is focus on what you can control: your mornings, your choices, your thoughts, your effort. Progress does not happen in leaps. It occurs in routines, small, imperfect, repeated routines.

PAUSE & THINK

What is one habit that feels good because it serves you, not because someone else expects it of you?

What kind of life are you building through your small daily choices?

How do your routines support the person you want to become?

> DISCIPLINE IS NOT ABOUT FIXING YOURSELF. IT IS ABOUT RESPECTING THE LIFE YOU ARE BUILDING. SMALL ROUTINES, CHOSEN WITH CARE, BECOME QUIET PROOF THAT YOU TRUST YOURSELF.

YOUR DISCIPLINE INVENTORY

1. List three habits that make you feel anchored.
Examples: a daily walk, stretching, journaling.
Write why each one matters to you.

2. Identify one area of resistance.
What is the habit you keep postponing and why?
Be honest.

3. Choose one slight shift to your 1% promise.
Not a complete routine overhaul.
Just a single 1% improvement.
Maybe replacing ten minutes of scrolling with breathing.
Consider drinking water before your first coffee.
Name it clearly: my 1% promise.

A SIMPLE ANALOGY

Think of discipline like a muscle. It grows through repetition and rest. Too much strain breaks it. Too little effort weakens it. Your twenties are not about lifting heavier, they are about lifting smarter, with intention.

RETURNING HOME
THE FREEZE FRAME

EVERY RETURN FEELS HEAVIER THAN THE DEPARTURE. The suitcase might be lighter, but the heart is not. Coming home after months or years away makes you want to step into a paused photograph, one that never stopped waiting for you. The streets look the same. The people look the same. Even the air smells like memory. But something has changed, you. It is like watching an old movie of yourself. You recognise the scenes, the voices, the rhythm, but you no longer fit the frame.

The hardest part of coming home is not reverse culture shock. It is realising that you have outgrown a version of your life that still exists. I remember walking through my hometown, passing familiar cafés, hearing the same gossip that used to fill weekends. People asked the same questions: "How was it?" or "Are you staying this time?" but none of the answers fit in a sentence. How do you explain to someone that you have changed when everything around you stayed the same? That is what coming home feels like: living, living proof that time moves differently in various places.

Home has a strange way of holding your past selves hostage. You walk into the kitchen, and suddenly you are sixteen again, arguing about curfews. You meet an old friend, and suddenly you are eighteen, dreaming about leaving. You sit on your childhood bed and wonder how you ever fit into this room, this town, this version of you. It isn't that the home rejected you. It is that it does not know who you have become. And maybe that is not its job. Friends and family do not always see the change. They still joke the same way, still repeat the same habits, still expect you to be the same person you were before. But when you have lived elsewhere, navigated new environments, cultures, failures, and identities, your perspective shifts. You start noticing things that used to feel normal but now seem loud, limiting, or small. That distance can be lonely.

THOUGHTS RUNNING FREE

Coming home feels like pressing play on a scene that paused years ago. Only now, you are the stranger in your own story. They stayed the same. You changed. And that is okay. Home does not need to recognise you to be a part of you still. You can outgrow it and still love it, just like you can move forward without leaving it behind.

You miss people but cannot always reach them anymore. Not because of miles, but because of the mindset. Coming home often shows not what is missing, but what is finished. It is easy to romanticise return: the comfort, the nostalgia, the reunion. But comfort can also trap. After experiencing independence living in a different house or living abroad, returning home can feel like surrendering freedom for predictability. The strange part is you still love it. The streets, the smell of home-cooked food, the small rituals that shaped you. But they no longer fill you, do not fill you anymore. They remind you of a version of yourself that you have gently outgrown. That is why coming home hurts. Not because home is bad, but because you have become too big for it.

PAUSE & THINK

What does "home" mean to you now? A place, a person, or a feeling?

Which parts of home still comfort you, and which confine you?

How do you carry your growth without needing everyone to understand it?

THE FREEZE FRAME TEST

Write down three things that stayed the same while you were away.
Then write three things that changed within you.
Ask yourself.

Do, do these still fit together? Or is it time to rewrite what "home" means now?

FOR RETURNING SOULS

Do not shrink to fit if you have grown beyond your old environment, honour that expansion. You do not owe familiarity to your smaller self.

Share stories, not superiority. People might not relate to your experiences, which is okay. Speak with humility, not hierarchy.

Let nostalgia visit but not stay. It is natural to miss the past, but you cannot build your next chapter in yesterday's house.

Create micro-homes everywhere: a coffee spot, a friend's kitchen, a journal, or a morning walk. Home can be rebuilt in pieces, wherever you are.

VIII
LESSONS AND LAUGHS

Growth through motion, reflection, and surrender. The twenties are not just chaos. They are comedy. Every mistake, heartbreak, and airport breakdown is part of growing up faster than expected. And learning to laugh about it.

TRAVEL AS FAST-TRACK MATURITY

TRAVEL OFTEN APPEARS AS FREEDOM: THE OPEN SKY, the escape, the promise of "finding yourself." People post sunsets and airport gates, but rarely the quiet weight behind them: the guilt of leaving, the ache of distance, the feeling of being both lucky and lonely at the same time. People leave for many reasons: work, love, opportunity, survival, and air that feels easier to breathe. Every decision to stay or to go carries its own kind of loss. Some feel trapped by staying. Others ache from leaving. Both are valid.

This year marks ten years since I first left home. Not forever, but for six months. My first real time away. I went on an exchange to Australia in grade eleven. At the time, I was already in a complicated long-term relationship. My first attempt to go abroad, a three-month program in Canada, had failed. I almost gave up. My mum did not. She worried I would become one of those girls who stay too long in a relationship, never see the world, and forget to become her own person. Her push became my permission. Leaving home at almost seventeen and figuring life out on the other side of the world felt intense and disorienting. The foundation of who I am today began there.

For me, travel teaches resilience. It strengthens connection. It builds soft skills and survival skills. And yet it leaves the elephant in the room: loneliness. Anyone who has travelled in their twenties has probably asked, "*Am I running away, or am I learning?*" Sometimes loneliness is not a warning sign. It is evidence of growth. I still remember sitting in a bus station, my backpack digging into my shoulders, exhausted. Part of me thought, What am I even doing here? Another part whispered, This is exactly why you came. That whisper mattered more

What was supposed to be six months abroad became a sequence of years that rewired how I see everything. In 2018, I started in Iceland. When the Canada plan collapsed, I drifted to the United States, stayed with people I had briefly met while working at Burger King, and eventually landed in Australia with no wallet, no plan, and more trust in strangers than I had ever had before. What began as disorientation became education. Travel accelerated lessons adulthood was already preparing to teach: patience, humility, improvisation, and the art of asking for help.

Travel always holds a duality: fascination and unease. It removes the scaffolding of routine. No family. No familiar streets. No automatic safety net. Without those anchors, people themselves become the structure. A delayed bus, a wrong turn, or a quiet night in a hostel dormitory becomes a classroom.

My first real culture shocks in Australia were not kangaroos or left-hand driving. They were small frictions: people mispronouncing my name "Lee" (instead of "Lea"), nearly missing my stage call at a school assembly because of it, uniforms, meat pies for breakfast, and slang that German school English never covered.

Ariah, my first Aussie friend, and her mum Jenny drove us to school most mornings. One day, I saw my first kangaroo and screamed so loudly she nearly swerved off the road. These moments did not look dramatic from the outside, but they quietly stretched my tolerance and flexibility. They taught me how to belong before I understood how.

Returning home after that first exchange felt almost as hard as leaving. In a small place, gossip travels faster than truth. I heard it all:

"She's changed."
"She's strange now."
"Does she think she's better than us?"

Travel forces you to grow up quickly, not because you become "better," but because life has shown you things others have not experienced yet. The hardest part is returning to your old life and realising you have grown while everything at home feels frozen in time. Sometimes jealousy and regret hide behind casual comments.

Those moments become turning points. You either shrink back to old expectations, or you accept that you have outgrown what once felt like home. What is home anyway? A place, a person, a rhythm, a feeling? Travel does not erase home. For me, it multiplies it. Home becomes a shared meal, a voice message, a song that makes you exhale in the middle of chaos.

Years later, travel tested me again, not as a teenager discovering freedom, but as a twenty-something trying to build a life in Australia. This time, the lesson was not culture shock. It was endurance. During a stay in Brisbane with my travel mate Stef, uncertainty reached its peak. I did not have a work visa. My money was running out. Even with generous friends, I felt untethered. One morning, sitting by the river while waiting to get to Bundaberg, I called a friend across time zones. Europe slept. He was awake. That connection steadied me.

Standing there, I realised I needed to stop forcing myself forward. I booked a flight home, not as failure, but as recalibration. The truth was simpler. I had grown, and growth rarely looks familiar. Travel stopped being about where I was going and started becoming about who I was when nothing else held me together.

Travel makes you raw, a more honest version of yourself. Every person you meet only knows the piece of you that you choose to share. That freedom feels liberating, but it also makes going back harder. You realise you have outgrown home, or at least the version of yourself that lived there.

Independence grows from walking around with your résumé, facing rejection, adapting, and trying again. Tolerance develops in small frictions: snoring roommates, endless queues, lost luggage, changing plans. Patience becomes practice. Perspective becomes peace. Travel turns into a crash course in adulthood. No syllabus. No teacher. Just the world as it is.

At first, travel feels like escape. Slowly, freedom turns into responsibility. When you are constantly moving, no one else is left to blame. Missed buses, lost money, wrong decisions all circle back to you. That is when travel stops being a vacation and becomes a mirror. Every city reflects a version of you: who you were, who you are, or who you are becoming.

Travel teaches through contrast. It offers independence but demands surrender. It gives beauty and exposes fragility. Patience through missed flights. Resilience through getting sick alone. Trust through strangers' kindness. Gratitude through small comforts: a clean bed, a warm meal, shared laughter. The deepest growth does not come from what you see. It comes from what you survive and how you adapt. Growth rarely announces itself. It arrives disguised as difficulty.

At some point, travel stops being about seeing more and starts becoming about feeling deeper. Studying sustainability in Sweden taught me systems. Living and working in Australia taught me people. The classroom explained change. Travel required me to live it. Over time, the photos mattered less. The lessons stayed. I hesitated less. I listened more. I trusted uncertainty slightly more than before. Movement became grounding. Loneliness became self-connection.

People ask, "Don't you want to settle?" Settling does not always mean staying. Travel shows that roots can exist in motion: in friendships across continents, in short-lived but meaningful encounters, in moments of belonging that appear briefly and stay deeply. Stability becomes an inner rhythm, not a fixed address.

Travel does not fix you. It does not erase fear, insecurity, or longing. It removes distraction. No roles. No routines. No reputation. Just you. In that exposure, uncomfortable or not, you see yourself clearly. That is why travel changes people. Not because of what they find, but because of what they face.

You start searching for answers.
You end by meeting yourself.

Travelling brings freedom and guilt. There are evenings when I imagine my parents wondering what time it is where I am. Missed birthdays. Conversations half-lived through time zones. Life at home continues without me. That continuity hurts and reassures at the same time. Sometimes guilt is not a sign of wrongdoing. Sometimes it is a sign of care. Roots remembering where they started.

THOUGHTS RUNNING FREE

I sat in a bus station, exhaustion on my shoulders.
What am I even doing here?
A quieter voice answered:
This is exactly why you came.
I changed.
They stayed the same.
Or maybe we just grew in different directions.
Movement is not running away.
It is returning to parts of yourself you have not met yet.

When I trace my longing for movement and horizon-wide thinking, it leads back to Sunday evenings watching documentaries with my parents. Bear Grylls. Steve Irwin. A grandfather who wrote books about distant places. A necklace from Namibia. Those stories taught me that curiosity is its own form of love. Sometimes I fear the ocean and still want to dive in. That tension defines travel. It does not elevate you above others. It changes how you see.

Travelling in your twenties is like a fast-forward to maturity. It compresses lessons life would teach you anyway: patience when nothing works, humility when language fails, adaptability when systems collide, and letting go when people become temporary but meaningful chapters. Travel does not just take you away from home. Over time, it teaches you how to carry home within you, into every country, every room, every version of your life.

TRAVEL DID NOT MAKE ME FREE. IT MADE ME REAL.

THE ABSURD MIDDLE BITS

NO ONE TELLS YOU THAT TRAVEL MATURITY IS BUILT in the in-between moments. Not the sunsets. The logistics. Like standing at an airport counter, confidently handing over documents you have triple-checked, only to be told you are missing one piece of paper you did not know existed. Or realising that the visa you researched for weeks expires exactly three days before your rent is due. Or discovering that "temporary" housing means living out of a backpack for long enough that you stop unpacking altogether. There were moments when adulthood felt less like growth and more like improvisation. Explaining your life story to immigration officers. Memorising passport numbers. Learning the art of nodding calmly while panicking internally. Smiling through jet lag, uncertainty, and the quiet thought of "*How did I end up here?*"

Airports became emotional checkpoints. Some departures felt powerful. Others felt like grief disguised as movement. I learned that crying in airport bathrooms is almost a rite of passage. So is pretending you are "just tired" when you are actually overwhelmed by how much your life does not resemble a plan.

There is also humour in the small humiliations: mispronounced names, wrong buses, showing up overdressed or underprepared, pretending to understand slang you absolutely do not. At some point, you stop correcting people. You let life rename you temporarily.

Looking back, these moments were not distractions from growth. They were the growth. The chaos. The awkwardness. The laughter that comes only after you survive the situation. Maybe the twenties are not about having it together. Maybe they are about learning how to laugh while everything is slightly falling apart.

THE ART OF LETTING GO

Letting go sounds peaceful in theory, but in practice, it often feels like breaking apart. Every journey, whether a trip, a relationship, or a season of life, eventually asks for release. You cannot keep growing and holding everything at once. Travel taught me that endings are not failures. They are quiet transitions between versions of the self. The airport goodbyes, the unread messages, the empty hostel bed the morning after someone leaves, all of it becomes a subtle training in detachment. You learn to hold things without gripping. You learn to love without needing to own.

For years, I thought strength meant endurance, staying until the last thread snapped. But sometimes the real strength lies in loosening your grip. Holding on too tightly often comes from fear. *Fear that you will lose meaning if you stop trying. Fear that letting go erases what was good.* But memories do not need your control to survive. What was real stays real, even when it no longer fits your present. There are people you'll never forget, not because they stayed, but because they changed you. Some places will always feel like unfinished sentences. And there are versions of yourself that deserve gratitude, not guilt, for who they had to be at the time.

THOUGHTS RUNNING FREE

I used to think letting go meant losing. Now I see it means trusting. Trusting that what was meant to stay has already arrived, and that what leaves only makes space for what is next.

Travel is a constant exercise in goodbye, or, as I would rather call it, farewell. I am very sure that you will meet twice in life, and hopefully more often than that. You meet people in hostels, on buses, in kitchens that smell like five countries at once. You share laughter, stories, maybe even love, then one flight later, it ends. At first, the impermanence feels cruel. But over time, you realise it is the very reason you value connection at all. Nothing stays forever, so everything matters more. Each departure becomes practice for life itself. To say thank you instead of why, to hold softness instead of resentment, to honour impermanence instead of fearing it. Letting go does not mean forgetting. It means no longer carrying what is not yours to hold. It is not cutting ties in bitterness. It is recognising that some paths only run parallel for a while. That does not make them wrong, it makes them human. Letting go is an act of self-respect. It says: I honour what we had, but I no longer shrink from keeping it alive. The truth is, not everything lost needs to be found again. Sometimes closure is simply peace in not knowing.

We often mourn people and places, but rarely the identities we outgrow. The dreamer who thought life would follow a straight line. The student who believed success had a fixed timeline. The lover who thought effort could save everything. Letting go means thanking those versions for carrying you this far, then allowing them to rest. Growth demands space. Every goodbye, every transition, clears room for something new to unfold.

PAUSE & THINK

What are you still holding on to that no longer fits who you are?

Which memory or person still feels heavier than it should?

How can gratitude replace resentment when you look back?

THE LET-GO LETTER

Please write a letter (no need to send it) to someone, someplace, or a past version of yourself.

Start with: "Thank you for..."
End with: "I release you with gratitude."

Then, if you wish, tear it up, burn it, or save it quietly, not to forget, but to free.

1. **Do not confuse closure with conversation.**
   Some goodbyes never get words, they get acceptance.
2. **Let endings soften you, not harden you.**
   Pain is proof you cared deeply, do not turn that into armour.
3. **Remember: release is a skill.**
   Like anything, it strengthens with practice.
4. **You are allowed to miss what you have outgrown.**
   Nostalgia does not mean regression, it is remembrance.

I KEEP EVERY VERSION OF ME IN MY SUITCASE, BUT ONLY THE LIGHTEST ONES MAKE IT TO THE NEXT FLIGHT.

TWENTY-SOMETHING SURVIVAL GUIDE

I REALISED THAT BEING TWENTY-SOMETHING IS AN in-between stage that no one prepares you for. You are old enough to know better, young enough to learn the hard way still, and constantly torn between craving stability and fearing routine. It is a decade of contradictions. You look around, and everyone seems to be moving at different speeds. Some are engaged, some are still searching, some own houses, and others live out of backpacks. But none of those paths defines success. They are simply different timelines. Surviving your twenties has nothing to do with having life figured out. It is about learning to stay grounded while everything around you keep shifting.

Some days feel like breakthroughs. Others feel like nothing at all. But growth rarely looks dramatic while it is happening. Most of the time, it seems like consistency: getting out of bed when you would rather not, sending one job application, cooking something green, or saying no when you used to say yes. These tiny wins form the architecture of resilience. They are quiet, unglamorous, and often invisible to everyone else, but they build strength day by day. Then I realised: No one is ahead. No one is behind. Everyone is improvising.

THOUGHTS RUNNING FREE

Being twenty-something is not about reaching clarity.
It is about learning to live gracefully inside confusion.
Maybe "having it together" is not the goal at all. Maybe it is knowing when to let go, when to rest, and when to start again.

Social media makes it look like other people live in a constant highlight reel, golden light, perfect plans, and curated milestones. But behind every polished post sits the same confusion you feel. Everyone doubts themselves. Everyone compares. Everyone overthinks. Maturity is not about knowing everything. It is about accepting that uncertainty is part of the design.

It is easy to measure your life by milestones: degrees, promotions, relationships. But meaning often hides in the quieter moments, cooking for yourself, walking home after a long shift, finishing something you were convinced you could not. I think that being twenty-something means learning to value rest without guilt. It means realising that pausing is not falling behind, it is recovery. It means understanding that discipline without softness leads to burnout, softness without discipline leads to burnout, and softness without discipline leads to stagnation. You do not need to earn the right to breathe. Comparison will always whisper that you are late to success, late to love, late to peace. But you are not behind.

You are living your own timeline, shaped by your own experiences. The milestones you admire in others might not even fit the life you are building. There is no finish line. There is no race. Just an ongoing process of becoming.

PAUSE & THINK

What small things help you feel human again?

How often do you pause without checking a screen?

What makes you feel safe enough to stop proving yourself?

THE "ENOUGH" LIST

Instead of writing a to-do list, write a done list.
Include every small act that carried you this week: laundry, texts answered, boundaries kept, meals cooked, tears allowed, sleep prioritised.
Look at it.
Say: **This was enough.**

CHECKLIST

Signs You are Doing Just Fine

(Even If It Does Not Feel Like It)

- ☐ You got out of bed, even when you did not want to.
- ☐ You ate something that nourished you.
- ☐ You reached out to someone or let them reach you.
- ☐ You said no without guilt.
- ☐ You laughed at least once this week.
- ☐ You forgave yourself for something small.
- ☐ You reminded yourself that healing is not linear.

1. **Romanticise the ordinary.**
   Light a candle for dinner, even if it is noodles. Make the mundane feel meaningful.

2. **Do one thing that grounds you daily.**
   Stretch. Journal. Walk barefoot. Anything that brings you back into your body.

3. **Find a rhythm, not a rigid schedule.**
   Routines demand perfection. Rhythms adapt.

4. **Stay curious, not cynical.**
   The moment you stop asking "why," you stop growing.

5. **Remember: balance is not fixed.**
   It is a series of tiny corrections, repeated every day.

You are doing fine. The twenties are not meant to be mastered, they are intended to be lived.

GOT OUT OF BED. ATE SOMETHING GREEN. LAUGHED ONCE TODAY. MAYBE SURVIVAL LOOKS A LOT LIKE LIVING.

LOOKING AHEAD WITHOUT FREAKING OUT

THE FUTURE IS NOT A DESTINATION, BUT A DIRECTION. But in a world obsessed with milestones, it's easy to feel like life is rushing by while you're still standing still. For years, I believed that peace would come once everything finally made sense, once I had the career, the clarity and the plan. But peace doesn't wait at the finish line. It begins the moment you stop trying to control what is still in the making.

We grow up with the idea that life will "*click*" at thirty. That we will finally feel like adults, finally know who we are, and finally understand what we are doing. But adulthood has no end point. It is an ongoing process. In your twenties, you learn to survive. In your thirties, you learn strategies. In your forties, you learn to surrender. None of these is better than the other. None of these can be rushed.

Most fears about the future are not fear, but a feeling of lack of control. We confuse uncertainty with danger, even though it is often just potential that is still unformed and waiting to unfold. Comparing your life to others' is like comparing novels by their chapters. Some stories start slowly. Some start chaotically. None are behind. They just have different paces.

After years of searching for answers, a strange calm sets in. It doesn't announce itself. It comes like an exhalation that you didn't realise you had been holding. One day you wake up and realise that you are no longer panicking about the next phase of your life. Not out of apathy, but out of clarity. Because once you act from values rather than fear, there is less to control. That is the real turning point in early adulthood: not having fewer questions, but no longer being afraid of them. Success is not a fixed goal. It changes as you change. At twenty, success may mean adventure. At thirty, balance. At forty, peace. The goal is not to "make it." The goal is to create meaning. And let's be honest, does anyone really know what they're doing? Some people just panic more quietly than others.

THOUGHTS RUNNING FREE

Growing older is not about losing freedom.
It is about gaining clarity. Adulthood is not a finish line.
It is an unfolding map, drawn one decision at a time.

Being in your twenties feels like living with 47 browser tabs open: one is frozen, one is playing audio you can't find, and one randomly asks if you want to have children. Maybe it's not time for a five-year plan yet. Maybe you should just live, learn, flirt with chaos, and slowly realise what's really important.

Peace is not a goal. It is a practice. Uncertainty is not a flaw in the plan. It is a prerequisite for growth.

PAUSE & THINK

What version of success have you outgrown?

Which goals were never yours to begin with?

When you imagine your future self, what do they feel like, not what do they own?

WHAT KIND OF GROWN-UP DO YOU WANT TO BE?

Rate 1–5 how much these resonate:

	1	2	3	4	5
I value freedom over stability.	○	○	○	○	○
I want my work to reflect my values.	○	○	○	○	○
I prefer experiences over possessions.	○	○	○	○	○
I define success by peace, not status.	○	○	○	○	○
I see aging as evolution, not loss.	○	○	○	○	○

SCORE INTERPRETATION
(this is what they learned):

5–10 | Explorer

Growth right now comes from exposure. Curiosity matters more than certainty. The task is not commitment, but experimentation.

11–18 | Balancer

Growth comes from alignment. Structure and freedom both matter. The task is choosing without abandoning curiosity.

19–25 | Sage-in-Progress

Growth comes from integration. Values guide decisions. The task is trusting lived wisdom without closing doors too early.

No score is better.
Each reflects a different season, not a final identity.

GUIDANCE FOR MOVING FORWARD

STAY CURIOUS.

Curiosity keeps perspective flexible.

LEARN SOMETHING NEW EVERY YEAR.

Skills age slower than fear.

CHECK IN WITH VALUES REGULARLY.

Growth is direction, not decoration.

DO NOT PLAN THE WHOLE STAIRCASE.

Take the next right step.

Remember: aging means participation, not decline.

THERE IS NO TIMELINE. ONLY A LIFETIME,
AND THE COURAGE TO LIVE IT YOUR WAY.

IX
THE TURNING POINT

Surrender, clarity, and the beauty of not knowing yet.

FEELING LOST VS. FINDING DIRECTION

I AM TELLING YOU, FEELING LOST DOES NOT MEAN failing. It simply means you are in between versions of yourself, the one that no longer fits, and the one not yet formed. Lostness is not a mistake, it is identity in the process of construction. Everyone reaches that moment when the plan dissolves, and clarity hides behind confusion. Sometimes it happens after graduation, sometimes mid-job, sometimes on a random Tuesday when life feels too quiet. The mind whispers, "What am I even doing?" and that question is often the beginning of something new. There were days when I felt like I was moving through fog, changing places, jobs, and friendships, but not feeling at home in any of them. Lost in airports, lost in thoughts, lost in life. But maybe "lost" just means moving. Disorientation often precedes direction

.

THOUGHTS RUNNING FREE

Lost in airports, lost in thoughts, lost in life.
But maybe lost means I am moving.

Every "wrong" turn shows perspective. Every ending creates space for redirection. Every delay becomes an invitation to slow down and listen. What makes being lost harder is not the uncertainty, but the pressure to have it all figured out. Direction rarely appears when demanded. It arrives quietly, in hindsight, through choices that did not make sense at the time but led somewhere true. Feeling lost does not always look dramatic. Sometimes it shows up as restlessness, irritability, emotional numbness, or a strange sense that you are watching your own life from the outside. The days blur. Food tastes different. Your routines stop grounding you. Even joy feels muted.

Feeling lost can look like:

- *overthinking*
- *oversleeping*
- *constant distraction*
- *sudden stillness*
- *wanting change but not knowing what*

None of this means something is wrong with you. It means you are shifting.

The feeling of being lost becomes even stronger when you compare yourself to others. On social media, it seems as if everyone else is progressing steadily, reaching milestones on time and building a stable life. But most people put on a brave face and hide their confusion. Everyone improvises more than they would like to admit. No one is ahead. No one is behind. Everyone finds their way at their own pace.

Sometimes you are not lost, just misguided. You are living a life that once suited you, but no longer does. A job that drains you, a city where you don't feel at home, friendships that no longer fit who you have become. Feeling lost is often a sign that something within you has outgrown your current situation. The body often senses a misalignment before the brain can explain it.

A tightness in the chest. Fear of work. Irritability over trifles. Constant exhaustion. The feeling of being "off" for no apparent reason. These are not weaknesses. They are signals. A gentle nudge: something needs to change.

The direction does not return with fireworks or a dramatic breakthrough. It returns slowly through small moments of realisation. A sentence someone says. An idea that sticks with you. A feeling that remains silent. And one day, almost without noticing, you realise that you are no longer lost. You are simply moving gently and steadily towards something that feels right.

PAUSE & THINK

What moments in your life have felt most "lost," and what eventually came from them?

When did confusion push you to grow in ways comfort never could?

What if being lost is not the opposite of being found, but the path toward it?

LOST IS NOT THE OPPOSITE OF DIRECTION. LOST IS WHERE DIRECTION BEGINS. IT IS THE PAUSE BETWEEN VERSIONS OF YOU AND THE PROOF THAT YOU ARE CHANGING.

THE LOST & FOUND JOURNAL

Write three moments in your life when you felt directionless. For each, list:

1. What happened?
2. What eventually came from it? A lesson, a person, a shift?
3. Finish the sentence: "If I had not gotten lost, I would have never..."

You will notice the dots connect just later than expected.

THE "RIGHT NOW"

When you feel lost, ask yourself:

1. What is one thing I know for sure today?
2. What is one thing I can let go of today?
3. What is one small thing I can do next?

Direction grows from small steps, not big answers. Stop searching for instant clarity. Look for what energises you, even slightly. Ask questions not to find certainty, but to stay curious.

Remember: movement creates direction. Even tiny steps count.

WRITING, DREAMS, AND WHAT'S NEXT

THIS BOOK BEGAN WITH NOISE, TOO MANY THOUGHTS, too many questions, too much of everything. I wrote to make sense of it all, to slow down the chaos in my head. Somewhere between the pages, something simple but liberating became clear to me: no one really has everything under control. Maybe that's the point.

Writing became my method of turning confusion into clarity, or at least into something honest that I could hold on to. Writing this book was like holding up a mirror to the chaos. It made me realise how much beauty there is in uncertainty. Maybe none of us are really crazy, maybe being human is chaotic and connected in ways we've forgotten. Every day is an effort, and some days just getting out of bed is a victory. That, too, is a win. Celebrate small steps. Allow yourself to be a little "crazy" in such a loud and overwhelming world. Life is hard, and yet we keep trying.

"If I'm crazy, maybe we all are. But maybe that's the point: being human has never been neat or rational."

Looking back on ten years full of lessons shows that growth is never linear. Every age, every chapter, every change brings its own chaos and clarity. The one message that keeps coming back is to be patient with yourself, with others, and with time. Be patient with your friends who are discovering life in different ways. Be patient with your parents as they learn to let go. Be patient with yourself as you build the life you want. There is so much time, and yet somehow never enough. As you chase the future, remember to hold on to the moment. Try to enjoy the in-between. Things will unfold in ways you cannot yet see.

Thank you for accompanying me through the confusion, humour, heartbreak and small revelations of life in your twenties. If any of this has stuck with you, even if it's just one sentence, then you've already proven that we're not alone in this.

This last page is to remind you:

- **It's okay if you don't know something.**
- **It's okay to change direction.**
- **It's okay to start over as many times as you need to.**

If I am crazy, maybe we all are. And that is the point: to be messy and still shine.

WHAT REPEATS, WHAT REMAINS

SIMILAR PATTERNS APPEAR UNDER DIFFERENT NAMES in various chapters. Overstimulation reflects emotional avoidance. Doom scrolling reflects delayed decision-making. The confusion of modern dating reflects a general communication fatigue. Homesickness goes hand in hand with identity fragmentation. Each topic points to the same tension: too much input, too little integration.

The recurring discomfort is not caused by immaturity or lack of discipline. It reflects a discrepancy between the human pace and today's expectations. Growth does not come from acceleration, but from selective attention. Clarity comes less from answers than from boundaries: what to engage with, what to leave unfinished, what to stop explaining.

As this book shows, life in your twenties is not defined solely by instability. It is characterised by an increased sensitivity to systems, relationships and internal contradictions. This sensitivity creates friction, but also discernment. What feels like lostness often serves as recalibration. The following concluding section does not end the journey, but gives it a new framework.

X

NOTES TO SELF

MAYBE THAT'S THE WHOLE POINT

BEING IN YOUR TWENTIES ISN'T JUST AN AGE. IT'S an attitude to life. A time when you ask questions louder than fear and learn to shine even when nothing seems certain. No one has everything under control. But everyone carries a light within them that is quiet, steady and stronger when shared.

For a long time, life felt like something that would begin later. After the right job. The right city. The right relationship. The right plan. Thoughts filled every gap. Peace felt conditional, like something that would come when everything finally made sense. Then something changed. Not because all the answers appeared, but because self-confidence became louder than doubt. The brooding subsided as actions began to align with values. Acting in accordance with one's values does not eliminate uncertainty. It eliminates self-deception. When truth leads the way, there is less to analyse. Happiness ceases to be an achievement and becomes a calmer state, a kind of embodied peace.

Your twenties are not a waiting room for real life. They are real life. The chaos, the new beginnings, the small successes, the heartache, all of this shapes a version of you that will eventually be able to look in the mirror and say: I trust myself now.

Growing up may not mean doing everything right. It can mean staying kind while everything changes. Loving gently. Forgiving slowly. Returning to yourself again and again, even when life constantly rewrites the script. Healing doesn't always look dramatic. Sometimes it looks like breathing more slowly, worrying less, and quietly choosing yourself.

There is no fixed schedule. No final version. No uniform

definition of success. There is only a series of moments – gentle and stormy – each of which shapes who you become. Still being there, still figuring it out, means still being alive, still being curious, still becoming.

THOUGHTS RUNNING FREE

Maybe we never really figure it out. Maybe we just learn to live gently with what is still unfolding. To laugh at the chaos. To trust the timing. To love the process. Because even when nothing makes sense, you do.

That may be the crux of the matter. Not having everything under control, but recognising the beauty in becoming. Trusting the timing, even when it feels wrong. Letting your light shine or fade exactly as it is.

Letting your light shine has nothing to do with perfection. It has to do with authenticity. Every honest, kind or courageous act adds brightness to your inner life and quietly illuminates the path for someone else.

This chapter is not a guide to being flawless.

It is an invitation to be real.

LIGHT MAPPING

Recall moments when you acted courageously, kindly, or authentically, even in small ways.
Write them down as light points:

- a boundary held
- a truth spoken
- an apology given
- a risk taken
- a day you showed up despite fear

These moments are proof that the light has been present all along.

MAYBE THAT IS THE WHOLE POINT: TO BE LOST, TO BE MESSY, AND STILL CHOOSE TO SHINE.

A LETTER YOU WILL READ LATER

THE CHAPTER THAT MAKES SENSE IN TWENTY YEARS. One day, this will feel softer. Not because it was easy, but because distance changes the weight of things. One day, you will look back on your twenties and wonder how you managed to cope with so much at once. The confusion. The urgency. The constant feeling that life was just beginning, even though you were already living it to the fullest.

Right now, it feels chaotic. Decisions overlap. Emotions contradict each other. Some days you feel full of possibilities, other days you feel unbearably still. You question yourself more than you trust yourself. You replay moments that don't deserve so much space. You imagine versions of your life that don't always last, ideas, paths, identities that flash and disappear again.

And that is exactly the point. You are building something without fully knowing what it is yet. This book was written from inside that mess. Not afterwards. Not once everything made sense. It was written as things unfolded, when certainty was far away and questions were louder than answers. That's why, when you read it in a few years' time, you won't remember every detail. You'll remember how it felt before clarity set in.

You will see how restless you were. And how brave that restlessness actually was. How often you changed direction, not because you were lost, but because you were listening. How much you cared. How deeply you felt. How intensely you lived. You might laugh at the things that once felt like emergencies. You might ache for the version of yourself who thought she had to have everything figured out by now. And maybe, just maybe, you will feel proud.

Proud that you kept going even when you didn't feel ready.

Proud that you took risks without any guarantees.

Proud that you allowed yourself to be uncertain instead of settling for a life that felt too small.

Proud that you lived fully, even when it was uncomfortable.

The chaos will look different then. It will look beautiful. Adventurous. Necessary. Like proof that you didn't sleepwalk through your twenties, but showed up for them, fully awake, even when it hurt. This book is not here to teach you how to get through your twenties. It is here to remind you, later, that you did. That you survived the uncertainty. That you became someone through it. Or that you are still becoming, because that part never really ends. Maybe one day you will read these pages at a kitchen table you cherish, in a city that feels like home, with a life that once seemed unimaginable. Maybe you will read it and think I had no idea how much was waiting for me. Or maybe you will read it in the middle of another transition and realise that becoming does not stop at any age. Either way, this book will hold a version of you that mattered.

The one who tried. The one who questioned. The one who felt everything.

The one who did not have it figured out and kept going anyway. If nothing else, let this be proof: Your twenties were not wasted on confusion. They were shaped by it.

LETTER TO YOUR FUTURE SELF

Write a letter to a future version of yourself at any age.
Include three parts:

NOW

Who are you in this moment?
What feels heavy?
What are you proud of?

LEARNING

What these years are teaching you about love,
boundaries, work, rest, and self-trust.

HOPE

How you want your future self to feel,
not what you want them to have.

End the letter with one question for your future self.
Keep this letter somewhere safe.
Return to it when life feels unclear.

END NOTE FROM ME TO YOU

If you have made it this far, thank you, for reading, for staying, for feeling along the way. Writing this book has been like holding up a mirror I wasn't always ready to look into. But maybe that is what twenty-something is, a lingering reflection you slowly learn not to run from.

I don't know where you are as you read this, on a plane, in your bed, between jobs, or between versions of yourself but I hope you found some versions of yourself in these pages. Not to offer answers but to create space for the questions we all are still asking.

I invite you to take a moment, to reflect on your journey and perhaps share your story with someone else. Your experiences and insights can offer comfort to others who are also finding their unique path.

If there's one thing I know now, it's this: figuring it out isn't something you finish. It's something you live. You will lose and rebuild, laugh at chaos, sit on your yellow bench, and keep meeting yourself in new ways. And that is beautiful because it means you're still becoming.

Where ever you go next, go gently. Trust that even when life feels uncertain, you are never truly lost.

With all my love,

Lea xoxo

P.s. If you close this book feeling less alone, it has served its purpose.

AFTERWORD

27 THOUGHTS I KNOW NOW

WHEN I STARTED WRITING THIS BOOK, I THOUGHT I would find answers. Instead, I found perspective. These are the thoughts that remained with the quiet ones who came back, even after the noise had subsided.

1. Everything feels impossible until you've already done it.
2. Growth rarely feels like growth while it's happening.
3. You can be happy and uncertain at the same time.
4. No one really knows what they're doing; some are just better at pretending.
5. Healing doesn't mean becoming who you were before, but loving who you are now.
6. "I don't know" is an honest answer.
7. Some people teach you gentleness, others teach you boundaries.
8. You can miss someone and still know they're not right for you.
9. Forgiveness doesn't mean going back, it means letting go.

10. Not everything that breaks apart needs to be fixed.
11. Time doesn't heal all wounds, but it helps you not to reopen them.
12. Sometimes the universe whispers through endings.
13. Self-confidence isn't loud, it's quiet self-awareness.
14. The people who feel like sunshine are the ones you should keep.
15. "No" is a complete sentence.
16. You will leave people, places, and even versions of yourself behind. That's okay.
17. You don't owe everyone access to your energy.
18. Overthinking is just love and fear fighting for control.
19. Silence is productive.
20. The present moment is enough; it's the only thing you really have.
21. You don't have to explain your peace to anyone.
22. Be gentle with people; everyone carries something invisible with them.
23. Most of the time you're not behind, you're exactly where you're supposed to be.
24. When something doesn't work, it makes room for something that will.
25. You don't need closure from others to start over.
26. The goal is not to have everything, but to have what is important.
27. It's not about finding answers, but learning how to live without them.

THOUGHTS RUNNING FREE

If you are reading this, you may already have recognised some things. Take a moment to reflect on a recent experience or lesson that has shaped you. Write down what you have learned from it and keep these insights handy. They will remind you that even in uncertain times, you are not alone on this journey, that everyone has such experiences, and that we all continue to grow nonetheless. Embrace the continuity of growth and the shared human experience of uncertainty. You are still becoming, still beautifully human.

THE FOUR LAWS OF FIGURING IT OUT

After all the brooding, crying, laughing, learning and new beginnings, I realised that growing up isn't about rules, but perhaps about memories. So I wrote my own.

LAW 1
NOTHING WORKS UNTIL YOU DO IT

You can manifest, plan or dream, but the universe will only meet you halfway. Show up, even if it's messy, even if it's small. Action is where alignment begins.

I remember a situation where I felt completely lost, surrounded by chaos. I was working on a project that overwhelmed me, so I started with the smallest task: tidying up my desk. It didn't solve all my problems, but it created a sense of order amid the mess and made it easier to take the next step.

LAW 2
FEELINGS ARE NOT FACTS (THEY ARE SIGNPOSTS)

Emotions are messengers, not dictators. They show you what has not yet been healed, not what is true forever. You don't have to believe every thought, you just have to listen long enough to understand it.

One simple way to process these emotions is to keep a journal. By writing down your feelings, you create a personal space to explore and reflect on them. Alternatively, talking to a trusted friend can provide clarity and insight, as they may offer perspectives you haven't considered. Both practices can form the basis for your self-reflection.

LAW 3
YOU CANNOT LOSE WHAT IS MEANT FOR YOU

People, jobs, opportunities – what is meant for you will always come back to you. Stop chasing. Start receiving. When something goes away, it makes room for something that is a better fit for you.

However, it is important to recognise that letting go is not always easy. It can be incredibly difficult and often requires time and patience. Understand that it is natural to struggle with this process and that it is okay to see this challenge as part of your journey.

LAW 4
YOU ARE THE CONSTANT

Everything else, the cities, the faces, the different versions of yourself will change. But you are the only one who goes everywhere with you, wherever you go. Learn to make peace with your own company. You are the home you have been searching for.

THOUGHTS RUNNING FREE

Maybe we never really "figure it out." Maybe we just learn to live gently with what is still unfolding. To laugh at the chaos. To trust the timing. To love the process. Because even when nothing makes sense, you do.

Take this moment as an opportunity to pause close the book for a moment, inhale deeply, and notice your breath. I invite you to embrace this uncertainty through a simple act today: sit with an unanswered question for five minutes.

Allow yourself to contemplate it without the need for immediate answers, and discover what insights or feelings emerge in that quiet space.

ACKNOWLEDGMENTS

A HEARTFELT THANK YOU TO BROOKE, WHOSE presence, wisdom, and gentle push shaped so much of this book. Our ENFJ–INFJ connection became more than a personality match, it became a balance of vision and grounding, emotion and structure. Thank you for listening to unfinished thoughts, for helping me find words when I could not, and for connecting me with Tayler, whose guidance helped this book become what it needed to be. You reminded me that creativity grows best in connection, and that the right people show up when you finally start speaking your truth.

To Tess, thank you for being my loudest cheerleader from the very first moment I mentioned writing this book. Your excitement never faded, not even for a second. Every time you said, "You recharge my soul," I felt it, and I believed it.

To the Tavern Team and everyone on the island, thank you for asking about the book week after week, for hyping me up during long shifts, and for reminding me that people were waiting for this to exist. Your energy, humour, steady encouragement, and quiet belief carried me more than you know.

To everyone who showed up quietly, consistently, and without expectation, thank you. To the people whose support did not announce itself, but revealed itself through reliability, shared space, late conversations, check-ins, and simply being there when it mattered most. You reminded me that some of the strongest connections are built not through grand gestures, but through presence.

Every flower that appears in this book was drawn by someone close to me — family, friends, and people I met along the way. Each one is a small symbol of growth, nurture, and becoming. Not everyone managed to draw a flower, still, each contributor knows which flower is theirs, and together they form a quiet pattern: seeds, soil, care, and light, much like the people who helped me become who I am.

Thank you to everyone who contributed a flower, shared excitement, encouraged me when I disappeared into hyper-focus, or inspired me without realising it. Without each and every one of you, this book would not have come together in the way it did.

This book was created for me, but also for you, for everyone who is still figuring it out. If you are reading this and recognise yourself somewhere in these pages, you are part of my story. You are the soil, the care, and the sunlight that helped this book grow. I invite you to stay connected, to share your thoughts, and to keep the conversation alive. This journey does not end here. It continues in connection, reflection, and the stories we are still becoming.

And to you, Brad, thank you for your patience and for bringing my vision to life.

ABOUT THE AUTHOR

I WAS BORN IN 1998 IN A SMALL TOWN IN GERMANY, but I never really felt like my life would stay within its borders. From early on, something in me wanted movement, distance, and perspective. After finishing school, I worked in hospitality, a job that looks simple from the outside but teaches you a lot about people. Long shifts, unfamiliar faces, quick connections. It taught me resilience, empathy, and how much can happen in brief moments with strangers.

In 2018, I left for the first time in a way that truly mattered. What started as a trip became a turning point. Iceland was my entry into the unknown: vast, quiet, uncomfortable, and grounding all at once. From there, the journey unfolded in ways I could never have planned, through unexpected friendships in the United States and moments that confirmed something I already felt deep down: openness changes lives. Years later, during a difficult hike in Iceland, I learned one of the lessons that now quietly shapes this book. Not everything needs to be controlled. Some things ask to be trusted, even when the path is unclear. That moment stayed with me more than any highlight ever could. Australia later became a second home. Sweden shaped my academic path through a master's degree in sustainability. Travel remained my most honest teacher. Over time, my idea of home changed. It stopped being a place and became a collection of people, shared moments, and familiar feelings found in unfamiliar spaces.

THOUGHTS RUNNING FREE

One small win, one brave decision, one moment of laughter, that is all it takes to keep hope alive.

This book grew out of too much thinking, too many questions, and the constant feeling of being in between. My writing blends reflection, philosophy, and a quiet sense of humour to capture what it means to be twenty-something: uncertain, curious, restless, and still becoming.

In my search for clarity, I discovered something simple: no one really has it all figured it out. And maybe that's the whole point.

PAUSE & THINK

Being twenty-something is not a destination, it is a process of becoming, of learning to live with uncertainty and still finding beauty in it.

“

You have found peace with the chaos, but you can still laugh about it.

”

Still Figuring It Out

www.ingramcontent.com/pod-product-compliance
Ingram Content Group UK Ltd.
Pitfield, Milton Keynes, MK11 3LW, UK
UKHW051206260726
13967UKWH00011B/3138

9 780646 733449